★ 1956

Jan 11 — At the RCA studio in Nashville, Elvis is paired with back-up singers The Jordanaires. Drummer D.J. Fontana joins the group on record for the first time. Together they record Mae Axton's song "Heartbreak Hotel."

Mar 24 — Elvis makes six appearances on *Show*, a CBS TV show prod Jackie Gleason.

March — *Elvis Presley* is shipped, event becoming Elvis' first Gold Albu.

April 3 — Elvis appears on the *Milton Berle Show* TV show. He sings "Heartbreak Hotel" and "Blue Suede Shoes."

April 25 — Elvis signs a three picture contract with Hal Wallis and Paramount Pictures.

June 5 — Elvis returns to the *Milton Berle Show*.

July 1 — Elvis, dressed in tie and tails, reprises "Hound Dog" on the *Steve Allen Show* to a nervous basset hound.

Aug 10 — In Jacksonville, Florida, Judge Marion Gooding warns Elvis that he must tone down his act.

Sept 9 — Ed Sullivan's show features Elvis for the first of three television appearances.

Nov 16 — Elvis' first film *Love Me Tender* premieres.

★ 1957

Mar 25 — Elvis purchases Graceland.

Dec 19 — Elvis is drafted to the US Army.

★ 1958

Mar 24 — Private Presley joins 12 other recruits on a bus to Fort Hood, Texas, for basic training.

disposition, Gladys
ed for an undiagnosed

s Presley dies.

Aug 15 — Gladys Presley's funeral.

Sept 22 — Elvis boards the U.S.S. Randall and sails to Germany.

★ 1959

Sept 13 — Elvis first meets 14-year-old Priscilla Beaulieu.

★ 1960

Mar 2 — Elvis returns from Germany.

Mar 23 — RCA's plant presses one million copies of Elvis' newest single. "Stuck on You"/"Fame and Fortune" is released with the title "Elvis' first recording for his 50,000,000 fans all over the world."

May 12 — ABC broadcasts Frank Sinatra's *Welcome Home, Elvis*, a TV special.

July 3 — Vernon Presley marries Dee Stanley.

Elvis
handbook

Elvis
handbook

Tara McAdams

MQP
MQ Publications Ltd

Elvis

Introduction

I came to Elvis Presley in a very roundabout way. By the time I was born, Elvis was out of the army and had already embarked on a series of films destined for weekend afternoons when there was nothing else on television. The easy, tepid charm that oozed out of those mindless dialogues did little for me.

If I saw the *'68 Comeback* I don't remember it, but I'll guarantee I rolled my eyes as my mom and grandmom commented on how good Elvis looked. He was part of the Tom Jones/Dean Martin/Bobby Darin school, built for the small screen and the twinkle in my mother's eye. Their charm—"charisma," they called it— immediately emasculated those Vegas guys in my eyes. Their songs were catchy, but irrelevant to my friends and I, caught up in our teenage secretions and romances and hatreds. These guys were smooth, hairless—like Ken dolls. Old Ken dolls.

By the time I got to college, Elvis had died. His coffin photo blanketed every supermarket line. The drug use, spending habits, stream of young girlfriends were public fodder, and everyone I knew had the photo of him with Richard Nixon, another hypocrite. Elvis was a joke, a punch line. "Thank ya very much," long sideburns, split pants, huge sunglasses—he was atomized into a million fragments and absorbed. Elvis was gone, man, real, real gone.

It wasn't until after I moved to Memphis that I started thinking about Elvis. It was the fans; their love for him was massive, poignant, weird, and uplifting. I became something of a meta-tourist, someone who hangs around the scene during Death Week. It was—again—funny, but something in my heart slowly turned.

Reviewing his movies for an anthology, I gained an admiration for him. The songs were pretty bad and the plots were worse, but Elvis was a real workhorse. Only a kid who'd had nothing could be convinced that money proved how much he was loved.

He was a combination of naïveté and mistrust that you find in the very poor and the very rich. Who else would give away Cadillacs but not pay a decent salary? Who else collected deputy badges for real? Prescription drug addiction fitted perfectly for a boy who thought doctors were gods and loved to get one over on them. I started to think about how the drugs made him a ghost, how he lost his sex appeal and his drive and his compassion, all the things that defined him. I imagined how he must have felt, in that freezing bedroom with the foil on the windows, watching television when Johnny Carson made a joke about him.

The way I really got to Elvis, though, was when I started to listen to his early stuff. "That's All Right," "Blue Moon of Kentucky," and "Mystery Train." His voice is more than beautiful; it's strange and loaded with risk. Even listening through the rock paradigm that he created and then fell victim to, you can feel how different he was.

When I think about Elvis now, about how I am older than he was when he died, about how sad and lonely he became, I think that I love him. And then I think how ridiculous that is. And then I think that if I met him, he would say that it was okay. And he would mean it.

Tara McAdams, Memphis, 2004

Note: All quotations are from Elvis Presley, unless otherwise indicated.

Mississippi

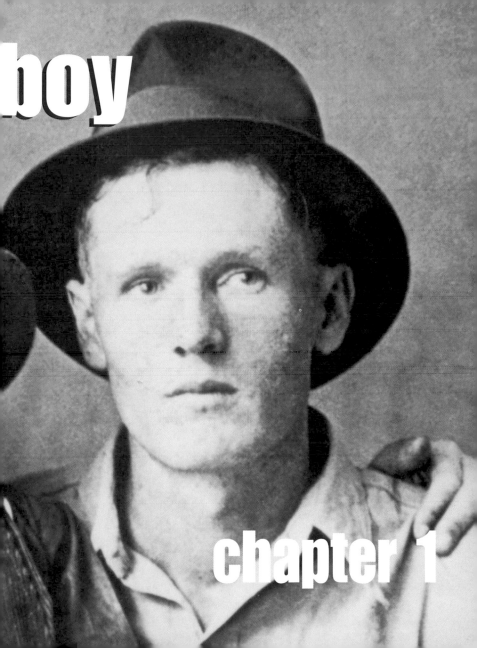

boy

chapter 1

A place of promise 1935–1954

Excluding a tiny manger in Bethlehem, the most famous birth place in the world may be a two-room shack in East Tupelo, Mississippi. At about 4:35 a.m. on the morning of January 8, 1935, Elvis Aron Presley came into this world. His birth was the happy ending to a very difficult labor; thirty minutes earlier, his mother had delivered a stillborn child—another boy, Jesse Garon Presley. Elvis' arrival surprised everyone but his mother; she had known she was carrying two children, though the doctor told her differently. All throughout his life Elvis would speak of Jesse. He and his mother would reputedly visit Jesse's unmarked grave many times throughout his childhood and Elvis was often reminded by his mother that "when one twin died, the one that lived got all the strength of both." From the beginning, then, Elvis Presley learned that he was more than one man.

Elvis also soon learned that he was even more cherished than the traditional only child. His mother, Gladys Love Presley, recovering with Elvis in the hospital while his brother Jesse was buried, realized that complications from her delivery meant she could never have another child.

It was a devastating blow to the young couple. Vernon Elvis Presley was a good-looking young man, well-meaning if directionless. He had already worked a series of menial jobs when he met Gladys Love Smith. At seventeen, he was smitten with the pretty dark-haired twenty-two year old. Gladys' vivacity and spirit contrasted well with Vernon's good-natured fecklessness. In 1933 the couple eloped to Pontotoc, Mississippi. Vernon added five years to his age and Gladys shaved a couple off hers on the license; their relationship was cemented.

They quickly settled in as newlyweds in East Tupelo. Orville Bean, a local dairy farmer for whom Vernon sporadically worked, loaned Vernon one hundred and eighty dollars for the lumber to build the house on Old Saltillo Road. It was the typical starter home in Mississippi during those post-Depression years—no ceiling, just a roof, an outhouse, and a water pump behind the house. Although East Tupelo was one of the first communities to be "electrified" by the Tennessee Valley Authority, the Presley home was lit by oil lamps.

Still, the future looked bright. Gladys had a job at the Tupelo Garment Plant that paid two dollars a day and Vernon was working at one job or another. When Gladys had to quit her job due to complications during her pregnancy, it was the first of a series of problems that ended in the tragic death of her first born. Gladys was a changed person after the birth.

In 1937, when Elvis was two years old, the Presley's world was again rocked. Vernon, along with Gladys' brother Travis Smith and a friend named Lether Gable, was charged with altering, and then cashing, a check. Vernon had sold a hog to Orville Bean (the man who had loaned Vernon the money for his first house). When Bean paid Vernon with a check for four dollars, Vernon felt aggrieved. In a rare fit of entrepreneurship, Vernon changed the amount to fourteen dollars. Mr. Bean was incensed. All three men stood trial, and Vernon was sentenced to three years at Parchman Farm, the state penitentiary.

Without Vernon, Gladys' hard times got harder. She was not then working, and couldn't make the payments on their East Tupelo home. After losing the house, she and Elvis lived briefly with Vernon's parents before moving in with cousins Frank and Leona Richards. Gladys got a job at the Mid-South Laundry. Family and friends recall the forlorn mother and child, Elvis sitting on a porch, crying bitterly for his father, Gladys often making the five-hour trip with her son to visit Vernon in prison. After several months, Orville Bean relented and sent a letter requesting the

suspension of their sentence. Vernon was released after serving eight months in prison.

The family was again intact, but Elvis recalled that his father was never quite the same: "My daddy may seem hard, but you don't know what he's been through." Gladys, as well, hovered even more fiercely over her home and her son, and Elvis bore the brunt of his parents' almost obsessive sheltering.

At age six, Elvis began school. In the fall, he attended East Tupelo Consolidated, a public school serving grades 1 through 12. The school was about a half mile from their house, across Highway 78. His mother walked him to school every day, their sheltered world ending each morning when Elvis entered the raucous environment that 700 pupils inevitably inhabit, resuming again each afternoon. The few people who do recall Elvis in elementary school remember him as an average student, a shy, quiet youngster, rather apart from the crowd and with few friends.

Vernon continued on a long series of short-term jobs. Although he always was either employed or seeking a job, he could never get his family's financial state solidified and, as a result, the family had to move repeatedly. But there was one place where the family had a foundation. Increasingly, their moral and social nexus was the Assembly of God church. Like many other small-town churches, music was the heart of the service, and of the congregation.

Music, whether it was gospel or country, was definitely central to the lives of the Presleys, as it was to many of the families in this area. And it was through music that a young Elvis Presley stepped out of the crowd for the first time—at the annual

Previous page: **Elvis' birthplace, Tupelo Mississippi, 1979**
The two-room "shotgun" shack which Vernon Presley built on Old Saltillo Road, Tupelo, where Elvis was born.

Mississippi–Alabama Fair and Dairy Show, on Children's Day, in 1945. The fifth grader had so impressed his teacher during a morning assembly with his rendition of the cowboy weeper "Old Shep" that Elvis was entered in the fair's radio talent contest. On October 3, 1945, Elvis Presley's voice rang out over the airwaves of WELO, a prominent local radio station. Wise enough to not tamper with success, the boy reprised "Old Shep." Standing on a chair to reach the microphone, unaccompanied by any instrument, Elvis' first public performance was a triumph. The memorable day, however, was not without its drawbacks, as Elvis recounted in a 1972 interview:

"They entered me in a talent show. I wore glasses, no music, and I won, I think it was fifth place in this state talent contest. I got a whipping the same day, my mother whipped me for something—I don't know, [going on] one of the rides. Destroyed my ego completely." The boy had tasted the sweetness of an audience's approval, and his adventure was just beginning.

The second musically significant event in Elvis' childhood was also intertwined with his mother's protectiveness. For Elvis' eleventh birthday, his parents gave him a guitar. He had wanted a bicycle, but Gladys couldn't bear the thought of her son being injured. She persuaded her boy that music was both safer and more enjoyable: "Son, wouldn't you rather have a guitar? It would help you with your singing, and everyone does enjoy hearing you sing." His two uncles—Vernon's brother Vester and Gladys' brother Johnny Smith—both taught Elvis a few chords, but it was his pastor at the Assembly of God Church, Frank Smith, who really helped him begin to play.

With his guitar in hand and his first public triumph under his belt, Elvis Presley stood firmly in the place of every dreamy pre-adolescent who would soon hear his music—he was a wannabe rock/country/gospel star. Wannabe? Boy, did he. From this point on, everyone's recollections of Elvis are invariably meshed with music. He was still a shy boy; Reverend Smith recalled that he had to push him to perform at services. But he was well received at the church, and his commitment to music was evident.

It was at about this time that Elvis encountered Mississippi Slim, a Tupelo musician born Carvel Lee Ausborn. Slim's younger brother, James Ausborn, was a classmate of Elvis' at East Tupelo Consolidated. Mississippi Slim hosted a weekly show, *Singin' and Pickin' Hillbilly* on Tupelo's first radio station WDIX. Every Saturday at noon, Slim would feature local musicians on this show. Elvis dreamed so hard of being one of these guests that he made it happen. He sang two songs, accompanied by Slim, and the excitement and thrill was enough to hook him. From then on he was constantly after James to go down to his brother's show, and, shyly but persistently, exhorted Slim to show him guitar techniques and chords.

Just as the boy may have begun feeling a sense of stability, Vernon once again couldn't make the payments on their house and the family was forced to move from East Tupelo to Tupelo proper. The social ramifications included Elvis entering a new school. The move from East Tupelo to Tupelo was geographically slight, but it felt like a thousand miles from the world the Presleys had known. There were lots of Presleys in East Tupelo, and Gladys, Vernon, and Elvis were fine, churchgoing folk in hard times. In Tupelo, however, they were just poor white trash. They moved to an apartment very close to an infamous neighborhood known as "Shake Rag," a black tenement known for producing its share of ministers and criminals, and later to a middle class house on North Green Street, one of the three houses designated for white people. The music emanating from the surrounding churches, homes, bars, and businesses was mostly black, and musicians such as Jimmie Lunceford and Earl Hines were performing at this time. Although Mississippi was still fiercely segregated, and Elvis' school was white, it's possible that Elvis' appreciation for "black" music was rooted here, an appreciation that would later make Elvis a dream come true for Memphis music producer Sam Phillips, who said, "If I could find a white man who had the Negro sound and the Negro feel, I could make a million dollars."

By the time Elvis reached seventh grade, his passion for music became evident at school. He brought his guitar to class almost daily. Reactions among his schoolmates were, to say the least, mixed. Some of the children (probably from the same families who regarded East Tupeloans with disdain) thought that Elvis' "hillbilly" music was ridiculous, corny, out of place; others admired his persistence and passion. Just how atypical it was for him to be fancying himself as a musician is evident by an incident in the eighth grade: a few toughs grabbed Elvis' guitar and cut the strings. But every bit as telling is the reaction of his other classmates: they got together and raised money so that Elvis could buy new strings. The incident foreshadowed the reactions that Elvis would soon raise throughout the country.

The next year, 1948, meant another move—and this time it was to the big city of Memphis. Memphis was not cosmopolitan by New York standards, but in the vast rural area that included the Mississippi Delta and such farming towns as Tupelo, Memphis was where the lights burned brightest. The Presleys' move was less of an arrival and more of a departure—there had been speculation that Elvis had got a girl pregnant, and that Vernon was fired from his delivery job for using the company truck to sell bootleg whiskey. In fact, the family had been planning the move for some time, and it's likely that they had finally had enough of Tupelo. In Memphis, not only was the town bigger, but so were Vernon's possibilities for better employment.

The Presleys were soon accepted into a two-bedroom apartment in the Lauderdale Courts, a government housing project under the aegis of the Memphis Housing Authority. Families could earn no more than $2500 per year in order to qualify as residents of "the Courts." But the Courts were more than anything else a place of promise, a place where the playing fields were even and where the merit of the individual lay in his efforts, not his lineage.

With the move to Memphis, Elvis found nourishing soil in which his roots could grow. At the Courts, he soon teamed up with new friends, including Buzzy Forbes and Paul Dougher, with whom he'd remain friends for years. At L.C. Humes High, as well, Elvis built a small coterie of friends, including George Klein, Red West, and others who would remain loyal to him for decades. He was not wildly popular, and he wasn't distinguished academically (mostly Bs and Cs); his most prevailing feature was how he lingered in the background, on the sidelines, just out of reach.

By day, he was a shy teenager who joined the school Army Corps and was a library volunteer, who loved the guitar and girls, but who never put himself forward. But it was his clothes that announced a new Elvis, an Elvis who would be center stage, whose every move made girls swoon, whose music would change the course of American history.

On June 3, 1953, Elvis Presley became the first person in his family to graduate from high school. Gladys and Vernon hung their son's framed diploma in a place of honor. On the morning of graduation, Elvis got a job at M. B. Parker Machinists' Shop. His pay was thirty-three dollars a week. He began work the next day.

One of the problems we … had with Elvis' music at that time was he was known as a hillbilly singer and most of us were just coming out of the big band era. Hillbilly just wasn't our thing during high school… He always seemed to be carrying his guitar with him whenever you saw him, so much so that when we would see other kids carrying guitars, we would laugh and sigh, "Oh no, not another Elvis!"

Billie Chiles Turner, high school friend

Though we had friends and relatives, including my parents, the three of us formed our own private world.

Vernon Presley

Left: **Elvis and parents, fall, 1941**

Vernon, Elvis, and Gladys outside their clapboard house on Maple Street, East Tupelo. The Presley family were noted for their insularity. Few were allowed into their inner realm. Elvis was, as most who knew them agreed, particularly close to his mother. They had a series of pet names for each other, and would communicate in baby talk. All throughout their lives together, and even after Gladys' death, Elvis worshipped his mother and she, in turn, adored him.

Interview with Harold Loyd

Born in 1931, Harold Loyd was a first cousin of Elvis, the son of Gladys Presley's sister Rheta Smith Loyd. During the 1970s, Elvis employed him for a time as a nightshift gate guard at Graceland.

Interview by Rose Clayton and Dick Heard, from "Elvis: By Those Who Knew Him Best," reproduced with permission.

East Tupelo, Mississippi, was just nothin', a wide spot in the road… It was very small, and a few people owned the better part of it. It was hard to get work unless you wanted to work in the fields.

Gladys [Smith] was twenty-one and Vernon [Presley] only seventeen when they run off to Pontotoc [Mississippi] to get married [June 17, 1933]. Most of the family was on Gladys' side, the Smith side, and you could almost throw a rock from one of their houses to the other. Gladys was younger than my mother, Rheta. They was sisters. Vernon and his relations and all the Smiths, we were all close and visited quite a bit and always helped each other whenever we could.

Vernon and his brother Vester, they always worked at somethin'. Sometimes they would have a little truck patch, you know, a little garden, and they did public work. The times was much harder on Vernon and Gladys than it was on my mama and father and us, because we lived on a farm. At least we had plenty to eat.

It was rough back in the mid-thirties after Elvis was born. We didn't have much of nothing. 'Course, being kids, you don't worry about where the next meal is comin' from, but I'm sure it was hard on all the parents.

Early on, my family lived on a farm, and we raised just about every darn thing we ate… We always had a hog to kill in the wintertime— plenty of chickens, thousands of eggs. Vernon and Gladys and little Elvis would come to visit. I remember a while before they'd get ready to go, my mother would go out to the smokehouse where we had our sausage hangin', cut off a big piece of ham, get 'em some sausage, jars of beans and things. She'd package it all up and give it to them. Be enough to last 'em maybe a week. We shared.

Gladys was a good mother and a good wife. She was like a second mother to me, but, of course, there was a very strong bond between her and Elvis after his twin was born dead. As I understood it, Gladys couldn't have any more kids. Somethin' happened to her during the childbirth, so that drew her closer to Elvis. She was so protective of him. If Elvis just whimpered, she would run to him. I always played with Elvis real gentle when he was a kid, 'cause I knew how Gladys was.

Above: **Elvis, aged two, with his parents, 1938**

Shazam!

Once Elvis learned to read, he developed a passion for comic books. Gladys reverently kept them in sequential order and ensured that no other children meddled with his collection. Comics are not too unusual an interest for a quiet, somewhat withdrawn boy, but seen in the light of how his life developed, the riotous colors and outsize adventures on these flimsy pages were clearly influential.

One of Elvis' favorite comics was the *Captain Marvel* series. Captain Marvel's adventures begin when Billy Batson, a homeless newsboy, is led down into a subway tunnel by a mysterious figure. A strange train appears which carry the pair to a subterranean lair. There, Billy meets the wizard Shazam, who reveals that Billy has been chosen as a superhero, a champion of good in this miserable world. He orders Billy to speak his name. When Billy utters "Shazam," he is transformed into a tall, handsome superhero in a red jumpsuit with gold trim, a short white cape, and a lightening bolt insignia on his chest. His eyes are bright blue and his hair is jet black; an ebony lock cascades down his forehead. He learns that he only has to speak the name again, and he changes back to Billy Batson. As the name is spoken for the first time, the wizard immediately dies. All of his power now resides within this young poor boy.

Right: **Six-year-old Elvis, 1941**

Elvis at around the time he began grade school, the 700-pupil East Tupelo Consolidated.

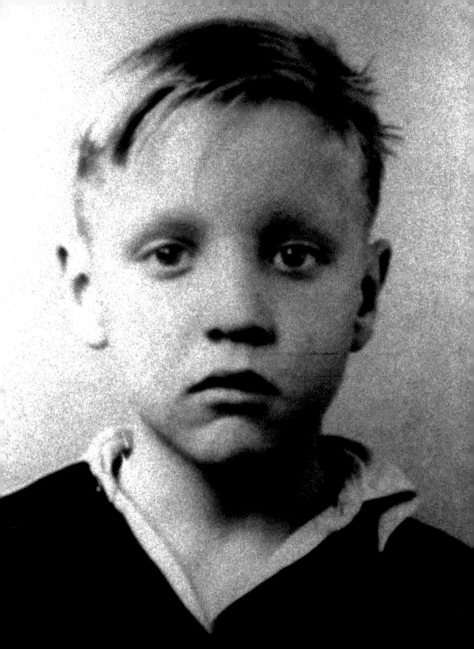

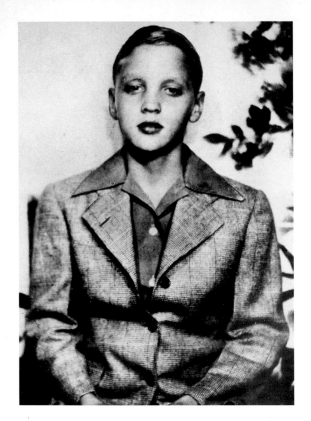

Above: **Elvis at eleven, Tupelo, 1946**

A studio portrait, possibly taken on Elvis' eleventh birthday, January 8, 1946, when he received his first guitar as a present from his mother.

Right: **Tupelo, 1948**

Thirteen-year-old Elvis in cowboy gear, not long before the Presley family moved to Memphis.

We were broke, man, broke, and we left Tupelo overnight. Dad packed all our belongings in boxes and put them in the trunk and on top of a 1939 Plymouth. We just headed for Memphis. Things had to be better.

Right: **Lauderdale Courts, Memphis, 1950**

A (toy) gun-totin' teenager, Elvis at fifteen, posing outside the Lauderdale Courts public housing project where the family moved in 1948 after leaving Tupelo.

Memphis music

Music was everywhere in Memphis. Elvis made trips to the Overton Park Shell to listen to concerts, to Ellis Auditorium, and the All-Night Gospel Singings, to the studio of radio station WMPS to listen to the *High Noon Round-Up*, featuring the Blackwood Brothers Quartet. Music wafted to his ears when he walked outside. Record stores on Main Street, a few blocks from his house, blared the latest sounds—Perry Como, Lightnin' Hopkins, Jimmy Witherspoon, Earl Scruggs. Elvis would have heard these as he made his way the mile or so to Beale Street, where blues artists like Muddy Waters, B.B. King, Jimmy Reed, Memphis Minnie, and others, could be heard playing in clubs— not only their records, but also musicians, live and in the flesh.

In Memphis, the radio was different. In addition to the country music, gospel, and pop to which he'd been exposed in Tupelo, he could tune his dial to WDIA, the nation's first radio station featuring a cast of announcers, all of whom were black, playing popular music for the African American audience. WDIA broadcast gutbucket blues, jumping rhythm and blues, hot gospel and cool jazz, all punctuated by the larger-than-life disc jockeys. When WDIA went off the air at sunset, WHBQ broadcast similar sounds. But this disc jockey was white, a manic record counter clerk named Dewey Phillips whose passion for the music was more powerful than his inability to operate the equipment; this technical handicap became a feature of the show, adding to the charming mayhem, which was Dewey Phillips.

If Elvis had powers laying dormant until the magic word was uttered, then so did Memphis. To the unpracticed or disinclined eye, Memphis was just a big hick town, unable to achieve the poise necessary to really be a city—corrupt, naïve, boisterous,

Above: **Beale Street, Memphis, c. 1955**

A vintage postcard shot of Beale Street, which—with its nightlife of jazz and blues venues—had been the entertainment hub for the local black community since the early part of the twentieth century.

racist, and rural. But Memphis had superpowers—you had to listen to Memphis. Music was in the air, part of the Memphis atmosphere. If a person chose to, he could breathe it. And Elvis, more than most, was panting.

Interview with Jim Blackwood of the Blackwood Brothers

Gospel group The Blackwood Brothers were a formative influence on the young Elvis who auditioned, unsuccessfully, to join a spin-off outfit, The Songfellows.

Interview conducted by Tom Graves in 2000 and reproduced with his permission.

I have an opinion about Elvis and his music that isn't too popular, but having known the man and talked to him numerous times over many years I feel I might be correct. See, I always thought that Elvis getting into rock and roll was really an accident. There is no doubt in my mind that Elvis' favorite music was Southern gospel music. He really loved singing those songs and he loved talking about the music.

The Blackwoods, we all remembered this shy Memphis boy hanging around backstage at the Ellis Auditorium. I remember one time in particular that he was hanging around outside the back entrance and he seemed kind of down. Well, I spoke to him and found out that he didn't have the money to buy the tickets for that night's "all night sing." I told him not to worry that I'd take care of it and I had a couple of tickets reserved for him at the box office. Well, he never forgot it.

It's no secret that he wanted to be one of The Blackwoods and auditioned for the young group Cecil Blackwood had started called The Songfellows. He wasn't chosen basically because Elvis was a lead singer and could not harmonize in the way necessary for a gospel quartet. Everything changed very rapidly after the plane crash that killed two members of our group. That was only a week before Elvis recorded "That's All Right." Right after the funeral in Memphis Elvis was picked by Sam Phillips to record for Sun. Elvis even called up my nephew, Cecil,

Above: **The Blackwood Brothers, 1960s**

The Blackwood Brothers, with (left to right) Cecil Blackwood, Bill Shaw, James Blackwood, Wally Varner, and J.D. Sumner.

and told him he couldn't sing gospel music anymore because Mr. Phillips had him singing the blues. If Elvis could have been one of The Blackwood Brothers, I think it might have been the only thing that would have made him leave from being the king of rock and roll.

I don't think there's any question that he liked the music he sang, I'm just saying that first and foremost he loved gospel music.

During our dating days, we had never gone anywhere to dance and it was not until we got to the prom, which was held in the Continental Ballroom of the Hotel Peabody, that Elvis told me he didn't know how to dance. So we sat out the entire evening—never dancing once! Later, I saw him in Jailhouse Rock on TV and I thought back to that evening and I said to myself, "I thought he told me he couldn't dance?"

Regis Wilson Vaughan, Elvis' high school prom date

Right: **Peabody Hotel, Memphis, 1953**

Regis Vaughan with Elvis, her date at the Humes High School senior prom. Elvis had dated fourteen-year-old Regis, who was a neighbor in Lauderdale Courts, through the spring of 1953. He borrowed a car and wore a brand new blue suit for the occasion.

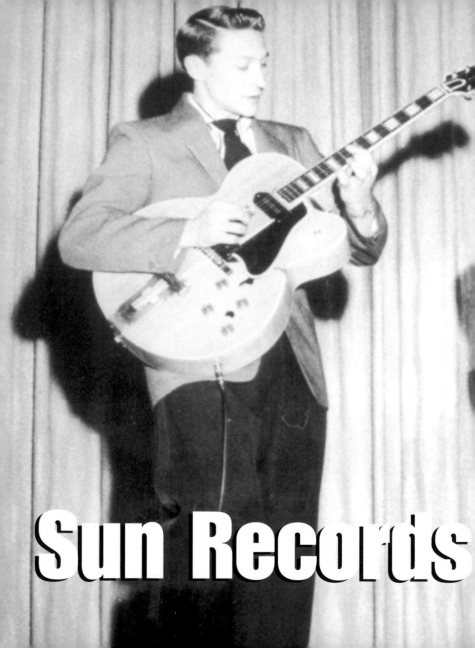
Sun Records

chapter 2

Elvis, Scotty, and Bill 1954–1955

In the summer of 1953, the eighteen-year-old Elvis Presley walked less than half an hour from his home into the tiny Memphis Recording Service studio at 706 Union Avenue, which was also the home of Sun Records. Ostensibly he wanted to record a song for his mother. At Sun, not only were professional records made, but anyone could walk in, pay out $3.98 for two songs and cut a real record.

Elvis brought the money and recorded two songs. If they were for his mother, the titles of these ballads told a little story, perhaps a reflection on his waning teenage years: "My Happiness" and "That's When Your Heartaches Begin."

Throughout that summer and fall, Elvis, who had taken a new day job at Precision Tools, returned repeatedly to Sun Studio, asking, always with the engaging diffidence that belied his persistence, if they had anyone interested in a singer. By January 1954, he cut another record with the songs "I'll Never Stand in Your Way" and "It Wouldn't Be the Same Without You." Two more songs. Four more dollars. No one could see the potential of Elvis Presley. Yet.

Elvis lived the life of a typical Humes graduate, working a series of menial jobs. He was nineteen, and involved in his first serious romance—fifteen-year-old Dixie Locke, a fellow congregant at the First Assembly of God church.

But the holding pattern that was Elvis' life was about to end. Scotty Moore was a local guitar player and band manager with ambitions to create a new sound. Sun proprietor Sam Phillips, impressed by his commitment, befriended him. When Scotty's country-swing group, The Starlite Wranglers, needed a vocalist, Sam suggested he give a listen to the anxious kid who'd been through Sun a few times. Elvis came to Scotty's apartment, and

Scotty brought in The Wranglers' Bill Black with his big stand-up bass. They fumbled through a variety of ballads, testing his rhythm with some Billy Eckstine, checking his feel with the latest from Eddy Arnold, letting him belt out Jo Stafford's "You Belong To Me." They decided to reconvene at the studio the next night, this time with Sam Phillips.

The session that was unfolding on the eve of July 5, 1954 seemed much like the previous night's rehearsal—anything but historic. They played some standards and a few pop numbers, but nothing was anything other than ordinary. During a break, while enthusiasm waned, Elvis saw his opportunity slipping away. Wanting nothing more than to lift their spirits and to inject some energy back into the session, he started an impromptu number, fooling around as he did at the Lauderdale Courts.

The song was Arthur Crudup's "That's All Right," and though it had been sung many times in many places, it had never, ever been sung like that before. With Bill Black slapping his bass and Scotty Moore streamlining the guitar, the song soared with the feral joy of youth. Elvis had intended to rejuvenate Bill and Scotty, and ended up creating a sound that would rejuvenate popular music. Elvis had found the portal. And Sam Phillips was relishing every minute of it.

Sam knew that everything had changed. He recognized the sound he had been waiting for, yet could not describe it. But now he had that sound on tape and, in his own pop culture laboratory, he could transform it into an acetate—a disc that he could supply to radio stations. If this disc was going to be jockeyed to the masses, there was only one disc jockey plugged into the mindset of the exciting, excitable kids who could see the same possibilities that Sam embraced in this new sound.

Sam Phillips and local D.J. Dewey Phillips—whose *Red, Hot & Blue* radio show was a Memphis institution—were related only by an obsession: the musical "moment" that transcends expectation. Dewey often stopped by Sun after his show, he and Sam talking music into the morning. Sam knew that Dewey was the only one who would "get" Elvis, and that, if he did, he was the one to deliver Elvis as well. Dewey knew a hit when he heard one, and if it wasn't a hit, he'd make it one.

And deliver he did. Dewey stopped by the studio and heard the recording that first night. The next morning, he requested two copies for his show. Elvis, unbearably nervous, fiddled with his parents' radio dial until it settled onto WHBQ's strong signal. Then, incapable of sitting still and waiting, Elvis ducked out of the house and went to the movies. Early in Dewey's show, Vernon and Gladys heard the name "Elvis Presley" surge into their living room. And so did much of Memphis. With that name came a new sound.

While the rest of Memphis was coming to terms with the fact that the quiet boy with the long sideburns and the dandyish attire had hit one out of the ballpark, Sam Phillips started working on the pitch. He quickly regrouped the musicians to search for a B-side to "That's All Right," and they came up with a sideways entrance into Bill Monroe's country hit "Blue Moon of Kentucky," a song as seemingly impervious to Elvis' colonization as Crudup's "That's All Right." But there it was—a black man's blues song and a white man's country song, both penetrated by a nineteen-year-old Memphian's unearthly rhythm and a record producer's vision. Rock'n'roll was born.

Sam pressed several two-sided acetates, and took copies to Dewey, and other important D.J.s: Bob Neal, host of WMPS' *High Noon Round-Up*, Dick Stuart at KWEM, and Sleepy Eyed John at WHHM. They all played the record—"Kentucky" was favorite—and Sam saw cogs beginning to turn. He knew Elvis would need a manager, and enlisted Scotty Moore. By the time

Sun Records #209 was pressed with the dawning logo and the rooster crowing, there were 6,000 local orders to be filled.

There was no time to waste. Within a couple of weeks Scotty and Sam put Elvis on stage at the Bon Air Club, where Scotty's Starlite Wranglers were playing. It was a hard drinking place with an appreciation for hillbilly songs and not for longhaired teenagers who were swirling Bill Monroe and Arthur Crudup in the same moonshine jar. Elvis played his two songs between the Wranglers' sets, with Scotty and Bill. He was too nervous to know how he'd done, and felt only disappointment in his first performance.

Seizing the chance, Sam got Elvis added to a July 30 show with Slim Whitman at the Overton Park Bandshell. Elvis' unease seemed to increase with his exposure. Before the show, Sam's assistant Marion Keisker took him to the *Memphis Press Scimitar*. Talking to a journalist, Elvis was instantly monosyllabic. The article ran without a single direct quote from the new star, instead quoting Keisker: "The odd thing about it," says Marion Keisker of the Sun office, "is that both sides seem to be equally popular on popular, folk, and race record programs. This boy has something that seems to appeal to everybody."

At the Shell, enjoyment remained elusive. "I was scared stiff," Elvis explained afterward. "It was my first big appearance in front of an audience, and I came out and I was doing [my first number], and everybody was hollering and I didn't know what they were hollering at." Nervous onstage, Elvis' legs had been shaking so badly that the movement was misinterpreted by the audience.

It might be hindsight, but girlfriend Dixie Locke seemed more aware of how momentous the occasion was than Elvis: "I don't think he was prepared for what was about to happen. He knew this was what he wanted to do and that it was breaking for him, but I don't think he [ever] thought everybody would just go crazy … he was doing something so totally *him*… And he loved it."

Above: **Sun Studios, Memphis, c. 2000**
The present day Sun Studio, with photos of its past around the walls.

The wheels kept spinning, slowly at first, fueled only by Sam Phillips' unyielding determination. He traveled from radio station to radio station—Houston, Atlanta, Shreveport. Many D.J.s were afraid of the Elvis record—afraid that its stylistic innovations would frighten their audiences. But fear is a vital part of revolution, and Sam continued to herald the new sound.

By day, Elvis was a mild-mannered driver of a Crown Electric truck, but by night a controversial insurgent. He returned to the Bon Air, and took on another small place called the Eagle's Nest; he made a brief radio appearance on KWEM in West Memphis; he even got reviewed in *Billboard* magazine, by the editor, Paul Ackerman: "a potent new chanter who can sock over a tune for either the country or the R&B markets." Scotty and Bill left The Wranglers on the strength of these gigs, throwing their full support behind the upstart. Over the summer they played regularly at the Eagle's Nest, as well as church rooms and social halls.

In August of 1954, "Blue Moon of Kentucky" entered *Billboard*'s Country and Western Territorial Best Sellers at #3. Sam Phillips was finally getting people to listen, including representatives from several large record labels. Finally, even Jim Denny of the *Grand Ole Opry* relented. This new music didn't appeal to him, but if the audience was putting it in the charts, he was willing to give "The Hillbilly Cat" a shot on the nation's premiere country broadcast and scheduled him for early October.

A world had opened up based on Elvis' first single, but they had not yet recorded a follow-up. Finally, in September, Elvis, Scotty, and Bill returned to Sun Studio. For an A-side, they came up with a thrilling version of "Good Rockin' Tonight," which had been a hit for R&B artist Wynonie Harris. For side B, they carefully wrought a carefree-sounding version of "I Don't Care If the Sun Don't Shine," a Mac Davis song popularized by both Patti Page and crooner Dean Martin, an idol of Elvis'.

Then they hit Nashville. For Elvis, the *Grand Ole Opry* was a dream he'd never dared imagining as a reality. The trio appeared at the famed Ryman Auditorium on October 2, and while the lyrics to "Blue Moon of Kentucky" were recognizable, the song itself was not, and they were received cautiously, if politely, by a traditional, non-teenage audience.

The *Louisiana Hayride*, a live radio show broadcast weekly from Shreveport, Louisiana, was an alternative to the *Opry*. With a signal of 50,000 watts, it reached twenty-eight states. And on the third Saturday of each month, CBS beamed the show for an hour on 198 of their stations nationwide. Elvis, Scotty, and Bill became regulars, driving eight hours from Memphis to Shreveport every Saturday. Between *Hayride* shows, the trio performed throughout the mid-South.

Following their *Hayride* debut, the boys quit their day jobs. The Tiplers, owners of Crown Electric, had supported Elvis' ambitions, appearing at gigs, praising him to friends and family. When Elvis left, Mr. Tipler was sad but understanding. Vernon and Gladys were more uneasy; the Memphis streets were littered with the debris of musicians' dreams, and for Elvis they wanted a solid future.

1955 began with promise. "Blue Moon" was still charting in *Billboard*, while "Good Rockin' Tonight" was making its own way up. Popular radio D.J. Bob Neal had taken an interest in Elvis. His domain was local, but he had been booking acts for long enough—including Elvis—to have connections beyond the city limits. The job was getting too much for Scotty, and in January 1955 Elvis signed a contract with Neal. One of Bob Neal's early pieces of showmanship was paying teenage girls to scream with abandon at Elvis' gigs, an expense that was soon unnecessary.

Elvis Presley had become a sensation—but a regional sensation. Bob Neal had set his eyes on the national stage, and was looking for someone who could get his boys there. By early 1955, he had found the answer: "Colonel" Tom Parker.

The truth about Parker is difficult to penetrate—was he Elvis' savior or destroyer? Without Sam Phillips' vision and determination, Elvis would have probably remained a delivery driver, his dreams receding as the years brought marriage and bills and children.

Colonel Parker had already shaped the careers of Eddy Arnold and Hank Snow, two country music stars. Elvis, however, was the Colonel's commercial masterpiece, a client willing to be shaped to the Colonel's commercial vision. The Colonel is a nexus where two Elvises merge. The shy, unworldly Elvis was overwhelmed by the Colonel's confidence; the genius Elvis was smitten with the Colonel's grandiose plans.

Parker's entrance into Elvis's career signaled a new level of finances, and that had a certain attraction to Sam Phillips. While a hit can be great for a small label, it can also wreak havoc, the demand for more discs draining finances while waiting for late paying distributors. Sam needed Parker, Bob Neal told him, and it was true.

Elvis, Scotty, and Bill returned to Sun to record "I'm Left, You're Right, She's Gone," bringing in a drummer—Memphis teenager Jimmie Lott. And across the south, Elvis was wowing every crowd he played to as his repertoire and experience increased.

To Parker, Elvis was a bankable investment. Elvis' parents were distrustful, by nature or necessity, and Gladys was also distressed to hear of the riots at Elvis' concerts. She worried for the safety of her only surviving son. But Parker's persistence and Elvis' confidence in him conquered their fears, and they signed the management deal. Elvis' career was now Parker's.

The Presleys left their apartment on Alabama Street, renting a two-bedroom home on Lamar Avenue. Girlfriend, Dixie Locke, was there almost constantly, she and Gladys consoling themselves with his nightly phone calls and his press clippings.

At Sun, the sale of Elvis Presley was looming. Sam Phillips was hesitant. He loved Elvis, he loved the *moment* of Elvis, that moment when something truly fresh happened. But he was low on funds and rich in new prospects. (Within months, Sun would release Carl Perkins' "Blue Suede Shoes" and "I Walk the Line" by Johnny Cash.) Parker, meanwhile, had his eye on RCA Records.

On November 21, 1955, a crowd gathered at Sun Studios. RCA executives, song publishers Hill and Range, Sam Phillips, Bob Neal, Tom Parker, Elvis, and his parents were all present. Elvis' contract was sold to RCA for an unprecedented $35,000. In addition RCA would pay all of Sun's back royalties to Elvis, who would now get a royalty of 5%–2% more than he got from Sun. With an added share in publishing royalties, it meant he would be a very rich young man. Six weeks later, Elvis Presley turned twenty-one.

This cat came out in red pants and a green coat and a pink shirt and socks, and he had this sneer on his face and he stood behind the mike for five minutes, I'll bet, before he made a move. Then he hit his guitar a lick, and he broke two strings. So there he was, these two strings dangling, and he hadn't done anything yet, and these high school girls were screaming and fainting and running up to the stage, and then he started to move his hips real slow like he had a thing for his guitar.

Bob Luman, country music artist

Right: **Sam Phillips and Elvis, 1955**
At Sun, Sam Phillips takes a guitar lesson from Elvis.

"Call Sam!"

The Memphis that you lived in and the Memphis that you listened to offered dual citizenship. You could walk the Memphis streets without ever being aware of this other realm. But there was one man who was giving out passports. No man inhabited the two worlds of Memphis as easily as Sam Phillips, perhaps because he, like many of the great names he was to record, was not a native Memphian. An engineer from Florence, Alabama, Sam grew up wanting to be an attorney, a man who would defend the downtrodden. But the law eluded him. Poverty-stricken himself, more pressing needs—food, money—demanded his attention. His career choice did, however, give the disenfranchized a voice; he came to Memphis and opened a recording studio at number 706 Union Avenue—Sun Studio.

Initially, Phillips established a reputation for recording "Negro" talent; he recorded local Memphis artists like Willie Nix and James Cotton, and was responsible for some of the earliest recordings of blues legends Howlin' Wolf, Bobby "Blue" Bland, and B.B. King. He sold these recordings to labels such as Chess and Meteor, but soon entered the business himself when he founded Sun Records.

In 1953, Phillips cut the hit "Just Walkin' in the Rain" by the singing group, The Prisonaires. The title was especially poignant considering that's just what The Prisonaires could not do; as residents of the Tennessee State Penitentiary, they were escorted by armed guards both to and from Sun Records.

The hit and resulting press brought Phillips and his studio some local attention. On his radio show, disc jockey Dewey Phillips (no relation) had been squawking "Call Sam!" whenever he thought a record was a hit, and after the newspaper article, more people knew what he was squawking about.

Above: **Sun Studios, early February, 1955**

Sam Phillips in the control booth at the Sun Studios, with (left to right) Elvis, Bill, and Scotty between takes at a recording session. The posed picture appeared in the *Memphis Press Scimitar* on February 5, 1954, and was probably taken just a couple of days earlier.

Right: **Backstage, Louisiana Hayride, 1955**

Elvis with broadcaster Horace Logan (left) and D.J. Ed Hamilton backstage at the Hayride. In October 1954 Logan announced Elvis on air with the introduction "Ladies and gentleman, you've never heard of this young man before, but one day you'll be able to tell your children and grandchildren you heard musical history being made tonight."

The other Mr. Phillips

Daddy-O-Dewey is best known as the first disc jockey to play Elvis Presley. But since 1949 when Elvis was fourteen, Dewey's popular "Red, Hot & Blue" radio program had been teaching Memphis kids to discriminate a good song, not a different color or religion. Dewey was everything that a D.J. in 1949 was not. He was not well-enunciated, certainly not dulcet-toned, decidedly not even-keeled. He did not program a predictable two-hour slot of country, pop, or light classical. Through music, he demonstrated that the boundaries of "normal" were arbitrary, and heralded a freedom that society feared. Many listeners took heart in the realization that they might be able, like Dewey, to parlay their own particular weirdness, oddity, or eccentricity into a career.

Dewey Phillips and Sam Phillips had become friendly through music. Many of the acts that Sam recorded got airplay and an important push on Dewey's radio show. Dewey played records by B.B. King, Howlin' Wolf, the Phineas Newborn Family; he played poker with Johnny Ace, and with Ike Turner he scouted talent for Sam's record label. At a time when sipping cool water from the wrong fountain on a hot day could cost a life, Dewey was making more than a musical statement.

By the time Sam Phillips cut his acetate of Elvis' first single in 1954, he knew who had the kids' ears. Dewey flipped when he heard it, and so did his audience when he broadcast it. Impressed by the music and the response, he sent for the kid himself. When Elvis showed up at the station, Dewey told him not to cuss, surreptitiously opened the microphone while pretending to spin a record, and casually began asking questions. When it was all done, Elvis asked, "Aren't you going to interview me, Mr. Phillips?"

Above: **WHBQ radio station, Memphis, c. October 1956**

Elvis revisits his Memphis champion Dewey Phillips at the WHBQ studio where the disc jockey had been the first to play his debut record.

Dewey broke many more artists and records, including Elvis' later RCA releases, as well as Carl Perkins' "Blue Suede Shoes" and Billy Lee Riley's "Red Hot" on Sun, Memphian Johnny Ace on Duke, and national artists such as Little Richard, Sister Rosetta Tharpe, the Dorsey Brothers, Bill Monroe, Little Walter, Nat King Cole, and Jimmy Reed. He listened to the spirit that was in the record, and not the stylistic genre. In addition to the Sun artists, Dewey was influential in shaping the careers of soul music stars on Memphis' Stax Records and other labels.

Riding high in late 1956, Dewey began an afternoon simulcast on radio and TV. *Phillips' Pop Shop* aired daily from 3:30 to 4:30 p.m., and the sucking sound heard at soda fountains around the city was not kids drawing on their straws but the after-school vacuum created by the rush of the kids toward their TV sets. Just as he'd done on radio, he broke rules on TV, creating rock and roll television. He immediately violated one of the cardinal rules of broadcasting, breaking TV's fourth wall—putting the cameras and their operators on the screen and making other technical operations part of the show. His power was such that for months WHBQ resisted network pressure to carry *American Bandstand* in that time slot.

Dewey had suffered car accidents, and the chronic pain led him toward pills, his unpredictability now becoming a liability. On a California visit paid for by Elvis, Dewey embarrassed his old friend on a film set by insulting the star, Yul Brynner. The last straw was when he stole a test pressing of "Teddy Bear," still weeks from release. Dewey began broadcasting it, hastening the release and terminating a valued and valuable friendship.

On September 28, 1968, Dewey went to sleep at his mother's house and didn't wake up. He'd helped bring musicians into this world, and musicians helped carry him out as pallbearers. As did Elvis, Dewey died at the age of 42.

About "Blue Moon of Kentucky": It was a mixture of black rhythm with a white man's country song, and it paved the way for the development of rock and roll.

Carl Perkins, Sun Records artist

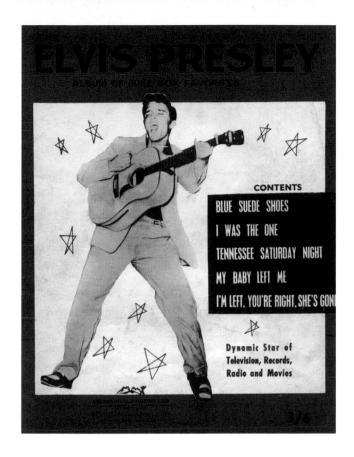

Above and left: **Tampa Florida, July 31, 1955**

The Tampa, FL performance (left) provided iconic photographs. One was used on his first album cover, and another (above) was used on popular sheet music.

Interview with Mae Axton

Mae Boren Axton was a publicist on Elvis' Florida dates in 1955. She later co-wrote "Heartbreak Hotel" with Tommy Durden.

Interview by Rose Clayton and Dick Heard, from "Elvis: By Those Who Knew Him Best," reproduced with permission.

When Elvis came to Florida to perform the first time, I met him and rode to the hotel with him. I had a deal with this friend of mine who had a beautiful hotel. It was really classy looking. The deal was that if the person I brought in could not afford their own room, I would give him a signal. I would just kind of lean over on the front desk as they were checking in, and the manager would know to bill that room to me. That way, no one got embarrassed. I didn't mind helping out some of those new kids. I was making pretty good money back then teaching school and doing PR and writing stories and songs, as well as promoting shows.

Well, anyway, Elvis called and I drove out to meet him. When I got there, I was kind of shocked. I don't know how their car ever got to Jacksonville. It didn't look drivable to me, but Elvis was proud of it. And there was not one kid, but three, Scotty and Bill were there with him. Bob Neal hadn't told me that Elvis was bringing musicians, and I could tell by looking at them that none of them had much money.

I said, "Elvis, you get in the car with me, and you two boys follow, and we'll go to your hotel." When we got there, you could kind of tell they'd never been in a place that pretty. They were a little uncomfortable. I told the owner-manager friend of mine, "They'll need a couple of rooms," and he let them fill out the registration forms. You could tell they were a little nervous. When they finished, Elvis said, "How much is it, Sir?" I kind of leaned up against the counter, and the manager said, "Oh, no, it's taken care of. Don't worry about it." Of course, he billed me.

Then I told them, "I tell you what, you get some rest, and I'll pick you up in an hour or so and we'll have dinner; then we'll go out to the show."

Above: **Tampa, Florida, July 31, 1955**

The date at the Fort Hasterly Armory was part of a package show headed by TV personality Andy Griffith. Elvis was at the bottom of an all-star country bill.

Then I called [singers] Skeeter Davis and June Carter and got them to join us. We had dinner and went on over to the show, and Elvis opened that night. Now Elvis' name hadn't even been in the ads, so no one knew who he was. I was counting money, and from the auditorium I heard all this loud screaming. That audience was going crazy over Elvis. I just couldn't believe it. I thought, "Boy, this kid's going to be a big star!" He wasn't even on the program!

I stopped checking the money to go down to see what all the screaming was about. This student of mine was standing up watching Elvis perform, and she was just going crazy over him—screaming, tears running down her cheeks. I tugged at her jacket, and she looked at me. I asked her, "What is it about this kid you like so much?" I think she gave the best definition of Elvis I've ever heard. She said, "Oh, Mrs. Axton, he's just a great big, beautiful hunk of forbidden fruit." I never forgot that.

We went on to Orlando the next night, and the crowds reacted much like the night before. Then the third night was in Daytona Beach. Early that morning I went out to do two radio interviews. When I got back to the motel I found Elvis sitting on the balcony staring out at the ocean.

He seemed so solemn. I asked him, "Are you okay?" He said, "Oh, yes, Ma'am. I just can't believe what I'm seeing. I've been sitting here for almost an hour, and I've seen three big ships go out there and just disappear." I said, "Yes, and probably a few thousand miles out there they'll still be on water, and they'll be coming into land again." He said, "I'd give anything in the world if I had enough money to bring my mama and daddy down here to see the ocean."

Following page: **Louisiana Hayride, December 15, 1956**

Elvis making a final guest appearance on the *Louisiana Hayride*, long after his one-year residency on the Shreveport radio show—which had been a major stepping stone in his career—had expired.

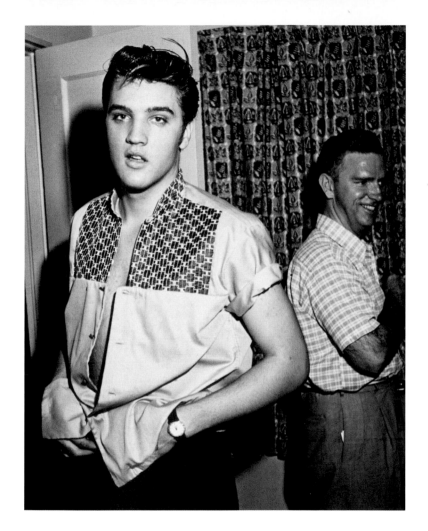

Above: **With Tom Diskin, c. 1955**

Elvis with Tom Diskin, who was one of Tom Parker's assistants and acted as Elvis' road manager. He was also Parker's brother-in-law.

Enter the Colonel

Colonel Tom Parker embodied just as much a paradigm shift as Elvis himself. "There had never been a manager of this sort before," Elvis biographer Peter Guralnick wrote. "In his attention to every aspect of his client's career, in his devotion to mapping out a program and to carrying it out in the most meticulous detail, in his use of radio for 'exploitation'…"

Mac Wiseman had Parker as his manager briefly: "Parker was ahead of his time. Back when he was managing (Eddy) Arnold, they had a sponsorship tie-in with the Purina company, and he had gotten Purina to sponsor or underwrite those Arnold shows. It gave them a tremendous advantage… Back then Parker did it just like those old boys do it today, with Wrangler and stuff like that. That's how far ahead of the game he was."

Tom Parker was born in Holland, and came to America at a young age. For a half dozen years he lived the footloose life in Tampa, Florida, then worked for the Tampa Humane Society, and founded a pet cemetery. Around 1939, he started working with country singers including Gene Austin and Roy Acuff. Parker was ready to enter the world of promotion with all the vigor and intensity of his previous ventures. He met Eddy Arnold, then an up-and-coming recording star, and signed him with a leading talent agency. He went on to book him in Vegas, get him on TV and into movies. At one point, wrote Arnold in his autobiography, he asked the Colonel why he didn't have a hobby. "He looked me straight in the eye and said, 'You're my hobby.' "

Parker obtained the faux honorific "Colonel" title from the singing governor of Louisiana, Jimmy Davis (composer of "You Are My Sunshine"). After Arnold fired him over a misunderstanding, Parker hooked up with Hank Snow, another country star. Again Parker focused intently on Snow's career, ensuring that Parker and his company, "Jamboree Attractions," managed Hank Snow Enterprises and all its commitments.

When Jamboree Attractions started managing Elvis Presley, Hank Snow quickly started feeling neglected. In a fit of pique he sold his half of the company to Parker, a bit too early, as Faron Young tells it: "Well, about a year or so later, Elvis Presley was the hottest son-of-a-bitch in the business. Snow went and got him a lawyer and was going to sue Parker. He wanted half of Presley and half of the company back. But the judge basically said 'You just made a bad goddamn deal.' Parker knew he was fuckin' Snow. He knew. But Snow didn't have enough sense to know it 'cause he was still like most acts—too vain. He was thinking, 'I'm the star.' Snow farted around and lost out on half of Elvis Presley. That's what he did."

The Colonel, and I don't mean it derogatorily, got dollar marks in his eyes.

Mae Axton

Following page: **Elvis and the Colonel**

"Colonel" Tom, his client, and their master: the RCA Victor dog logo, not long after they signed to the media giant.

Shoppin' for clothes

The area where Elvis really attracted attention was his clothing. Given that friends described him as shy, Elvis' attention to his appearance was remarkable. Most of his contemporaries' concerns lay with fitting in, with being a part of the teenage social order—an order that has rules and regulations more oppressive than any army. Elvis broke those rules. By his junior year his hair was eye-catching, greasier, more impenetrable than any other boy's. His friend, Ronnie Trout, remembers Elvis going through boxes of donated clothing at the Poplar Street Mission, searching for dress pants and shirts that would make him stand out, sometimes to his detriment:

Anytime anyone was different, people would make fun of them. They would do that with Elvis because of the way he dressed. He would wear dress pants or a shirt open at the collar to school. He would take a scarf and fashion it like an ascot, tie it like a movie producer. Then he'd wear a sport coat, like a one-button coat that looked like a zoot suit. All the other guys were wearing denim, T-shirts, loafers, moccasins, things like that. Elvis stood out. When you do that, you're asking for it, especially in North Memphis at Humes High School.

Elvis also began patronizing a famed clothing store, Lansky Brother's Mens' Shop. Lanksy's was famous for its bold styles and high-end African American clientele. Elvis' patronage, however, only extended at this time to the front window. Bernand Lansky recalled the boy's fascination:

Above: **Elvis with Bernard J. Lansky, Beale Street, c. 1955**

Elvis buying clothes at Lansky Brothers in Memphis' Beale Street. Lansky became known as "Clothier to the King" after Elvis shopped at his store in his youth—"I looked up one day and saw this young man looking at the displays" he was to recall years later.

When Elvis started working at the Loew's theater, he used to walk down to the corner on coffee break and look in the window... Elvis would stand there looking, and I'd say, "Come in and let me show you around." Elvis laughed and said, "I don't have no money, but when I get rich, I'll buy you out." I said, "No, don't buy me out, just buy it from me."

Bernard Lansky

Right: **Portrait, c. June, 1957**
Elvis redefined teen attire almost single-handedly. Touches like the upturned collar were adopted by young people around the world, among both boys and girls. In England it became part of the already established "teddy boy" look.

Big time

chapter 3

The rock'n'roll years 1956–1960

Now that RCA had bet the farm on the Memphis kid, they were anxious to see the crop. Having paid such a substantial price, the record company was eager to get Elvis into the studio. Steve Sholes, who directed RCA's artist and repertoire department and whose job was on the line, lost no time in getting a session together at the company's Nashville studio. Chet Atkins, the famed country music guitar master and a lifelong hero of Scotty Moore's, was an executive with RCA's Nashville office, and he was present both to supervise and to play. For the first time drummer D.J. Fontana joined Elvis, and he would continue to anchor the group's rhythm into the next decade. Elvis was seeing the inside of only his second recording studio, where he first attacked Ray Charles' "I Got A Woman." Then Elvis brought out "Heartbreak Hotel," a song from Mae Axton, the Florida promoter who had become one of his earliest supporters. She predicted he could make it a million-seller.

While readying the song for release, RCA capitalized on its new investment, releasing Elvis' most recent Sun single, "I Forgot to Remember to Forget" on their label. With better distribution it hit the charts for eight weeks, reaching the number one position. The kid was beginning to smell like money.

The Colonel had Elvis where he wanted him—on an internationally strong label. Next, the Colonel needed to create demand for those records via television. TV was ready for Elvis, and NBC's *Perry Como Show* lost its bid to *Stage Show*, a CBS variety show. Show promoter Bill Randle remembered how Gleason stood up for the king-to-be:

"Jackie Gleason loved Elvis. Gleason was half-stoned, sitting up there watching the monitors, and he said, 'That kid's pretty good. Have him do that one about "I've got a woman." ' Gleason literally changed the show schedule right then and there. And let me tell you, CBS had never heard anything like that before."

"Heartbreak Hotel" was released in late January 1956 and, just as Mae Axton had predicted, was a million seller by April 2. Elvis' first album, *Elvis Presley*, became RCA's first million selling album. By the time of Elvis' fifth and final appearance on *Stage Show*, he was confident and at ease in front of the cameras.

Elvis took time out on the way home from *Stage Show* to visit a friend. Carl Perkins was recovering from an auto accident that had smashed his dreams of performing on the *Perry Como Show*, opposite Elvis. "Blue Suede Shoes" which was written and performed by Perkins, was competing with "Heartbreak Hotel" in the charts—but Elvis and Carl were Sun brothers. Later Elvis would provide succor in a more substantial manner, recording his version of "Blue Suede Shoes." It would sell more than 12 million copies, creating a nice publishing nest egg for Perkins.

The day after Elvis arrived home from New York, he boarded an airplane and flew to California. The Colonel had arranged a screen test with Hollywood veteran Hal Wallis, who had produced masterpieces such as *Casablanca* and *The Maltese Falcon*.

Elvis' earnestness, his wild popularity, and the ease with which he'd adapted to TV won over Wallis. With the door a little bit open, the Colonel pushed and he secured a three-picture deal. Pleased, but never sated, the Colonel shrewdly avoided an exclusive contract, leaving opportunity open.

Next came more TV—this time the higher-profile *Milton Berle Show,* playing to sailors and their girlfriends on a special set on the deck of the USS *Hancock*.

From there, Elvis resumed touring. Ticket sales skyrocketed. Even Vegas beckoned. But first of all, he returned to Nashville to record "I Want You, I Need You, I Love You" with The Jordanaires. Their sound hearkened back to Memphis' gospel shows, and The Jordanaires became a regular part of his recording outfit.

On May 15, Elvis opened the week-long Cotton Carnival festivities in Memphis, headlining the Ellis Auditorium, a room he knew well from the audience's perspective. He brought out The Jordanaires as back-up singers, and unleashed the still unrecorded "Hound Dog," tearing the house down.

Elvis had a six-day break in his schedule, the longest since the start of the year, giving him time with his parents—and his fans. Elvis had bought his parents a new home—a ranch house in East Memphis. From dawn to dusk, people gathered at the front of the Presley home, hoping to catch a glimpse of the star. He often met with the fans, signing autographs and appreciating their enthusiasm. Having maintained such a hectic schedule, Elvis was unable to slow down. Fortunately, he ran into June Juanico, a girl he'd dated in Biloxi, and he had someone to whom he could show off his adopted hometown.

From Memphis, he flew to California for his second appearance on *The Milton Berle Show.* His boyish charm pushed "Uncle Miltie" to avuncular heights, who ruffled Elvis' hair and shouted to the audience, "How about my boy? How about him?"

Steve Allen, the hipster performer and singer noted for his square glasses and cool gaze, was not gonna play uncle. Though he signed Elvis for an appearance on his show, Allen was mindful of the scathing reviews the upstart was generating in mainstream publications. NBC announced, "We think the lad has a great future, but we won't stand for bad taste under any circumstances." So, coaxed into a white tie and tails, a neutered Elvis Presley sang "Hound Dog." *The Ed Sullivan Show* sniffed that the singer was "not their cup of tea"—though behind the scenes they were negotiating with Colonel Parker.

The real prophets were at RCA the next day—young girls

waving signs that greeted Elvis with "We Want the Real Elvis!" Elvis strode into RCA's New York studio bolstered by their support. After mastering the song live, it was time to record "Hound Dog." It took thirty-one takes. "Don't Be Cruel" took twenty-eight takes as Elvis strove to achieve the kind of breezy affectionate feel that comes across in the master take.

Next, he hit Hollywood. *The Reno Brothers*, as *Love Me Tender*, was originally named, was a Civil War potboiler. He arrived on the set with the entire script memorized.

Perhaps because Elvis was such a neophyte, and perhaps because Hollywood was exercising the same caution that Steve Allen did, Elvis' character had none of the raw, sexy Elvis; it focused instead on the sweeter, more diffident Elvis. Elvis was worried about his fans' reaction to his character dying in the end, but was reassured by his girlfriend June that "no one forgets an unhappy ending." He hoped she was right.

In Hollywood, Elvis had been quick to make friends, including actor Nick Adams, whose friendship with the late James Dean and a minor role in *Rebel Without a Cause* gave him instant cachet. Other members of Hollywood's hip crowd who befriended the boy wonder were a young Dennis Hopper and Natalie Wood. At the end of filming, when Elvis returned to Memphis, Nick and Natalie came to visit. A child star who was well used to celebrity, Natalie Wood was awed by the magnitude of Elvis' following, but found Elvis himself bland. Later she told her sister, "He can sing, but he can't do much else."

Life was flying by. December 1956: Elvis was home for the holidays, cruising down Union Avenue in Memphis, and passing Sun Studio when he saw a gaggle of Cadillacs parked out front. Inside he found Sam Phillips cutting a session with Carl Perkins, and was introduced to Sun's newest contender for the Elvis crown—Jerry Lee Lewis. Jerry Lee was playing piano on Carl's session, and when Elvis interrupted, they began jamming at the piano, singing spirituals and fooling around with some of the day's hits. Sam Phillips called in Johnny Cash—and a newspaper photographer. Sun producer Jack Clement rolled tape, the flash bulbs popped, and history was made—The Million Dollar Quartet forever captured at the height of their youth and power.

Less than a month later, Elvis was back in Hollywood. Elvis' second film, *Loving You*, was the story of a young country singer propelled to superstardom. It featured his first on-screen kiss (with the actress Jana Lund), a newly dyed crop of jet black hair (Tony Curtis was one of Elvis' film idols), and a much more relaxed Elvis. Gladys and Vernon, in LA to see their boy at work, ended up as extras, clapping enthusiastically as Elvis rocked out.

Elvis was making a movie, and Vernon and Gladys were making a move. Their East Memphis home had become too vulnerable to fans. Shopping for homes, Gladys asked the young realtor if they had anything "colonial." Graceland, an estate on more than 18 acres, had been put on the market only days before. Gladys was enchanted and, upon his return from Hollywood, so was Elvis. Never one to negotiate, Elvis quickly met the asking price, and purchased Graceland for a cool $102,500.

In May, Elvis returned to Hollywood for *Jailhouse Rock*—the film this time. Songwriters Jerry Leiber and Mike Stoller, who had provided Elvis with two previous songs on *Loving You,* were commissioned to write the soundtrack.

The film had a big dance scene and the choreographer, Alex Romeo, based routines on Elvis' own special rhythm. One of the sequences that resulted (from the number "You're So Square Baby, I Don't Care") was such a success that a popular flip book using the dance steps was produced.

Slowly but surely Elvis' life was being choreographed as well. The Colonel was ever watchful, and more controlling. Manager

Bob Neal had become victim to Parker's "reorganization." And Elvis' bandmates were not sharing in his new wealth. The trio's original deal, a 25-25-50 split, had become a flat salary when the money got good: $200 per week when working and $100 when not working. The camaraderie was fading.

Longtime girlfriend June Juanico had become sick of watching Elvis parade a series of starlets and showgirls through the news. She was replaced by Memphian Anita Wood, a petite blond who had recently won a beauty pageant.

Elvis' insularity increased. The adoration of his fans, though heartening, made his public life increasingly difficult. He began to cocoon himself with friends he could trust and depend upon. The Colonel tolerated no erratic behavior, so friends such as Dewey Phillip were pushed from the inner sanctum. Instead, friends like Red and Sonny West, Cliff Gleaves, Lamar Fike, and George Klein would increasingly accompany him. More would join his famous entourage—some were honest allies, some were little more than lackeys waiting for a hand out—most were a little bit of both. It was the beginning of the Memphis Mafia, and the end of any possible normal life for Elvis.

In December of 1957 Elvis got another booking—this time from Uncle Sam. Elvis picked up his notice at the local draft board, stopping by Sun studio soon after. Barbara Pittman, a fellow artist at Sun, remembered Elvis' private reaction: "Elvis cried in my lap because he had to go into the service. Parker had said, 'Look, son, you're going in. You play the hero. If you start battling it and try to get out of it to support your mother like some of them did, it's going to make you look bad. Just be the good ol' boy, the All-American-kid type.'"

The draft board granted Elvis a sixty-day deferment so that he could finish his fourth film, *King Creole*, where he worked with veteran costar, Walter Matthau.

On the morning of March 24, 1958, Elvis Presley was at the draft board, ready and publicly willing to offer his services to the United States Army. To the reporters' questions Elvis replied that he was looking forward to the army as a "great experience."

The next day, photographers were on hand to document Elvis' latest costume change. Dressed in army fatigues, he underwent what is arguably the most famous haircut in America, though he had to be called back to pay the 65 cent barber's fee.

Then to Fort Hood, Texas, where Colonel Parker and all press were ordered off base. Private Presley was now, for the first time in two years, on his own. He quickly adapted to his new life, acquiring his marksman and sharpshooter's medals. His country boy charm and modesty quickly won over fellow recruits, and he was named acting assistant squad leader.

With the weekends to anticipate, Elvis did well in the army. Soon Gladys and Vernon, accompanied by Vernon's mother (whom Elvis called "Dodger"), set up a house in nearby Killeen.

While Elvis thrived, Gladys did not. As the summer wore on, her health became fragile. A call to her doctor in Memphis led to a quick return home by train. She was hospitalized immediately, her condition grave. A frantic Elvis tried repeatedly to get leave, but for once his status worked against him; the army couldn't appear to favor him. A stern rebuke from Gladys' doctor, however, did the trick, and not a moment too soon. Elvis rushed home to his mother. She seemed to rally, and Elvis stayed until midnight. But at 3:30 a.m., the phone rang. "I knew what it was before I answered the telephone," said Elvis. Gladys was gone.

Even those closest to Elvis were shocked at the depth of his sorrow. Cousin Harold Loyd remembered his visit to Graceland:

"He said, 'Everything I have is gone—everything I've ever worked for. I got all this for her and now she's gone. I don't want any of it now.' It was real sad."

It was a somber Elvis who boarded the train for New York on September 19. Two things sustained him on his journey. The first was a book, *Poems That Touch the Heart,* given to him by a fellow soldier. The other solace came in the person of Charlie Hodge, also a new recruit, a fellow southerner, and a singer. Hodge, touched by Elvis' plight, kept up a stream of jokes and songs to buoy their spirits.

In New York, before shipping overseas, the madhouse again descended. Press, photographers, movie cameras, were all on hand to document his departure. Ever accommodating, he walked up the plank to board the U.S.S. *Randall* not once, but eight times, with a duffel bag borrowed for the occasion, so that every photographer could be satisfied. Three of the interviews were compiled and released as a recording; *Elvis Sails*, amazingly, went to #2 on *Billboard*'s charts.

The *Randall* landed in Bremerhaven, Germany on October 1, 1958, and Elvis became part of the 32nd Tank Battalion, Third Armored Division. On land the soldiers boarded a troop train to Friedberg; they would be stationed at nearby Ray Kaserne.

Several days later, Elvis' personal battalion of family and friends arrived in Germany. Since Vernon and his mother were financial dependants of Elvis, by army regulations Elvis was allowed to live off base with them. They moved into a house with five bedrooms, a large living room for entertaining, and a wary landlady who insisted on living with them.

Despite the private dentist and barber and special dermatology appointments, when Elvis was on base he was a regular Joe. He was promoted to acting sergeant in January, receiving his full sergeant's stripes a month later. Preparations were being made for home. He'd been overseas for eighteen months. Now Elvis faced another journey.

> I remember when I was nine
> years old and I was sittin' in front
> of the TV set and my mother had
> Ed Sullivan on, and on came Elvis.
> I remember right from that time,
> I looked at her and I said,
> "I wanna be just ... like ... that."
>
> **Bruce Springsteen**

Right: **Nola Studios, NYC, January 28, 1956**

Elvis and Scotty seen in morning rehearsals for the Dorsey Brothers' *Stage Show;* it was broadcast live from the nearby CBS Studios at 8 p.m. that evening.

Everything happened so blame fast I don't know where I was yesterday and I don't know where I'll be tomorrow.

Left: **New York City, December 1, 1955**
After signing to RCA, Elvis and the Colonel were flown to New York for this series of publicity shots. The "Heartbreak Hotel" sessions followed soon after.

I didn't know there were any radio stations in Nova Scotia. The more they try to ban the stuff, man, the more they'll have to listen to. I mean, a lot of people like it, man. It's hot right now.

Elvis, on hearing of a Halifax, Nova Scotia radio station that gave all it's Elvis records away so it didn't have to play them anymore.

Left: **RCA Studios, Nashville, April 14, 1956**

Prior to a morning-long recording session, RCA producer, Steve Sholes, presented Elvis with a gold disc for the song "Heartbreak Hotel." The event was duly photographed for a *Life* magazine story on the sharp rise to fame of this Memphis singer.

Above and following page: **RCA Studios, Nashville, April 14, 1956**

Elvis shed his jacket and shoes during the arduous three-hour session that only produced one number, "I Want You, I Need You, I Love You," this being in the days when three or four tracks would normally be produced in that time. Those

involved included backing vocalists Ben and Brock Speer, plus Gordon Stoker
without his regular Jordanaires, star country guitarist Chet Atkins, and RCA
man Steve Sholes, who is on the left of the dejected-looking group overleaf.

Thick-lipped, droopy-eyed and indefatigably sullen, Mr. Presley, whose talents are meager but whose earnings are gross, excites a big section of the young female population as nobody has ever done.

The New Yorker

Left: **Hal Wallis, Hollywood, April 25, 1956**

After some tricky negotiations with Tom Parker, the veteran movie producer Hal Wallis signed Elvis to Paramount Pictures in a deal—subsequently rewritten on even better terms—which would pay the star $100,000 for his first film, $150,000 for the second, escalating up to $200,000 for his third picture.

Right: **Backstage, Memphis, May 15, 1956**

Looking disheveled backstage at the Ellis
Auditorium in Memphis—and little wonder.
Elvis was topping the bill at the annual Cotton
Carnival, over the established country star Hank
Snow, and was greeted with wild enthusiasm by
the capacity hometown crowd. His frantic set
inevitably included his million-seller, which he
introduced as "Heartbreak Motel."

Above: **1034 Audubon Drive, Memphis, 1956**

Vernon and Gladys with Elvis, outside the first home they owned in Memphis.
It was located in a smart suburb, and Elvis bought it in the first flush of
superstar success, April 1956.

Above: **103 Audubon Drive, Memphis, 2002**

Compared to previous homes, Audubon Drive (seen here in 2002) was the height of luxury for the Presleys, soon to be eclipsed by the palatial Graceland.

Following page: **Elvis' bedroom, Audubon Drive, 1956**

Elvis relaxing in his bedroom at Audubon drive, where the family lived for less than a year until he purchased Graceland, March 1957.

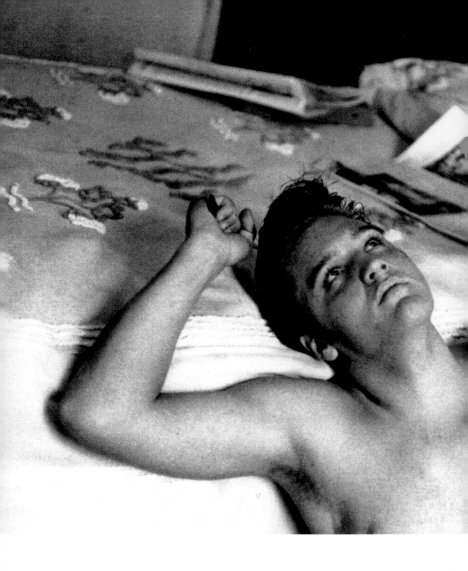

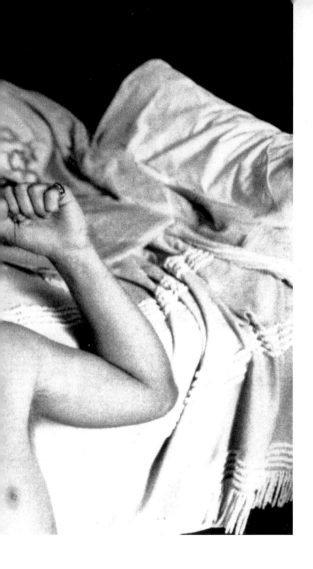

Debut in Vegas

Las Vegas in 1956 was a world of its own, powered by mob money and over-the-top artifice. Vegas was shiny pinky rings, gambling, and 17-piece orchestras cushioning the clatter of silverware. A twenty-four-foot cutout of Elvis greeted the boys when they arrived, but Elvis was soon cut down to size. In the Venus Room at the New Frontier hotel, when the group launched into their first number, according to promoter Gabe Tucker a voice rang out from a prominent table, "Goddamn it, shit! What is all this yelling and screaming? I can't take this, let's go to the table and gamble." Suddenly, Elvis was a long shot.

Even if he didn't gamble, Elvis was game, bravely finishing his two-week stint. Two short shows a night left Elvis, Scotty, Bill, and D.J. plenty of time for sunbathing, girl watching, and other adventures. He got Liberace's autograph for his mother, and even clowned around with "Mr. Showmanship" during one of his performances. It was on this trip to Las Vegas that Elvis saw Freddie Bell and the Bellboys perform "Hound Dog," and he added the song to his repertoire. Keenly aware that he was out of place there—*Newsweek* magazine described him "like a jug of corn liquor at a champagne party"—Elvis was unfazed: "Man, I really like Vegas. I'm going back the first chance I get." And he would. It would take more than a decade, but when he returned, Vegas would love him.

For now, it was back to the teenage girls, to the South, to the world that screamed *for* Elvis.

Right: **Las Vegas, April 1956**

Elvis takes it easy by the swimming pool of the New Frontier hotel during his Las Vegas debut, about which he later confessed, "It was awful … I wasn't getting across to the audience."

The booking was pretty mish-mash ... I don't know what the management expected of the kid. He wasn't prepared for doing a Las Vegas show. The songs weren't right for the crowd, his clothes weren't right, he had no production.

Comedian Shecky Greene, above Elvis on the New Frontier bill

Previous page: **Liberace and Elvis, May 1956**

Even if Elvis wasn't going down well with his Las Vegas audience, he was an attraction to the many celebrities—including piano star Liberace—who dropped by his dressing room for a photo opportunity.

Right: **Elvis and fan, Las Vegas, April–May 1956**

Despite the muted response to his Las Vegas debut, which ran from April 23 to May 6, Elvis took to the desert mecca of entertainment and gambling. *Variety* magazine reviewed one of his shows, concluding, "For teenagers he's a whizz; for the average Vegas spender, he's a fizz." Here he demonstrates some of his moves to a teenage fan.

Above and right: **The Milton Berle Show, June 5, 1956**
The Milton Berle Show, fronted by the man known as "The Father of Television," was rivaled on US TV only by that of Ed Sullivan. Following his appearances on the lower-profile Dorsey Brothers' *Stage Show* early in 1956, Elvis hit the nation's screens via "Uncle Miltie" in April, followed by a sensational return performance in June. On the latter show, Berle presented Elvis with a *Billboard* award for "Heartbreak Hotel" reaching number one on the retail, disc jockey, and jukebox charts in both the pop and country listings.

Elvis would sign autographs after shows, until it was physically impossible to do so any more, for his own safety as much as that of his fans.

Above and right: **The Steve Allen Show, Hudson Theater, New York City, July 1, 1956**

An awkwardly formal Elvis wearing a black tuxedo that was presented to him by the seemingly cool but fundamentally square host. The low-point in an embarrassing show came when Elvis had to sing his new show-stopper "Hound Dog"—which he had yet to record—to a bemused basset hound.

Left: **Russwood Park, Memphis, July 4, 1956**

By mid-1956 Elvis was red hot. His Independence Day gig, two years after first recording "That's All Right," followed his Steve Allen broadcast, when he'd worn a tux and sung to a canine. Elvis told the local fans, "You know those people in New York are not going to change me none. I'm gonna show you what the real Elvis is like tonight."

I can't figure out what I'm doing wrong. I know my mother approves of what I'm doing ... if I had a teenage sister, I certainly would not object to her coming to a show like this.

Left: **Florida, August 1956**

Elvis' TV appearances fueled a national moral outrage. The print media was already rampaging, and churchmen like Baptist preacher Robert Gray of Jacksonville, Florida, warned their congregations about the perils of local Elvis appearances.

Love Me Tender

Elvis' first movie was a western set at the end of the Civil War. Although the film was a straightforward drama, the producers still managed to contrive four musical spots for the new rock'n'roll sensation taking the lead.

Studio: 20th Century Fox
Released: November 1956
Producer: David Weisbart
Director: Robert D. Webb
Format: Monochrome/Cinemascope
Leads: Richard Egan, Debra Paget, Elvis Presley

RICHARD EG

EL

LOVE

CO-STARRING
ROBERT MIDDLETON · WILL
with MILDRED DUNNOCK · BRUCE BENNETT
Copyright 1956 20th Century-Fox Film Corp.

Above: **Still from Love Me Tender, 1956**

In Elvis' first film, he learned to ride horses, becoming a screen cowboy like the heroes of his youth.

Right: **On location, August–September, 1956**

During location shooting, Elvis rang Dewey Phillips in Memphis, telling him it was hard work—he'd spent all day behind a horse-drawn plow!

The Ed Sullivan Show

In the midst of filming *Love Me Tender*, the Colonel, in his efforts toward market saturation, landed Elvis his first appearance on The Ed Sullivan Show. On September 9, 1956, a record 60 million TV sets (82.6 percent of the television audience) watched Elvis' grand entrance into America's living rooms. Sullivan was recovering from a near-fatal car accident, so it was up to actor Charles Laughton to announce Elvis as they cut away to Hollywood. His performance of "Hound Dog" was drowned out by the screams that every move aroused. He took off his guitar for his next number, announcing his upcoming film and the ballad by the same name. He performed "Love Me Tender" with The Jordanaires, then rocked through "Ready Teddy," and "Don't Be Cruel." There was no attempt to censor Elvis during this performance, but the ecstatic screams that greeted him were soon joined by roars of disapproval—notably from the New York Catholic priest who condemned Presley as a "moral injury" and scorned this "voodoo of defiance and frustration."

Sullivan recovered from his accident and hosted Elvis' October return, and also his last appearance on January 6, 1957. The controversy over Elvis prompted Sullivan to issue a mandate: Elvis could only be filmed from the waist up. When Elvis started to move to Little Richard's "Ready Teddy," the camera amputated Elvis below the chest. Home audiences could only imagine what the Pelvis was doing, but the screams from the studio audience fed their fantasies. Nonetheless, Sullivan was also a convert to the Southern charm that exuded from Elvis, declaring, "This is a real decent, fine boy. We've never had a pleasanter experience on our show with a big name than we've had with you... You're thoroughly all right."

On the Sullivan program he injected movements of the tongue and indulged in wordless singing that were singularly distasteful... When Presley executes his bumps and grinds, it must be remembered by the Columbia Broadcasting System that even the twelve-year-old's curiosity may be overstimulated.

Jack Gould, New York Times

Previous page: **The Ed Sullivan Show, October 28, 1956**

Elvis chats with Ed Sullivan while preparing for his second appearance on the prime-time coast-to-coast television show.

Right: **The Ed Sullivan Show, September 9, 1956**

Elvis in action on his sensational debut appearance on the New York-based Sullivan show, his segment being broadcast live from Los Angeles.

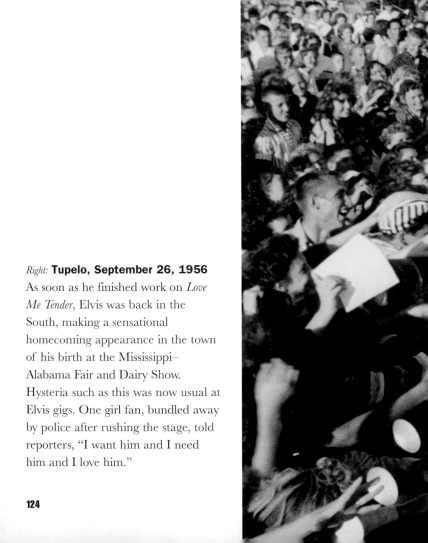

Right: **Tupelo, September 26, 1956**
As soon as he finished work on *Love Me Tender*, Elvis was back in the South, making a sensational homecoming appearance in the town of his birth at the Mississippi–Alabama Fair and Dairy Show. Hysteria such as this was now usual at Elvis gigs. One girl fan, bundled away by police after rushing the stage, told reporters, "I want him and I need him and I love him."

He's a real pixie and has a wonderful little-boy quality.

Natalie Wood

Left: **With Natalie Wood, Memphis, October 31, 1956**

While filming *Love Me Tender* Elvis got to know some of the young Hollywood crowd, including the actress Natalie Wood, whom he subsequently brought to Memphis for a three-day visit over the Halloween holiday.

Mr. Presley's first screen appearance ... is likely to leave most patrons untouched outside of the sizable circle of the singing guitarist's fans. For the picture itself is a slight case of horse opera with the heaves, and Mr. Presley's dramatic contribution is not a great deal more impressive than that of one of the slavering nags... But one thing you have to say for him—he certainly goes at this job with a great deal more zeal and assurance than the rest of the actors show.

New York Times, on Love Me Tender

Left: **Times Square, NYC, November 15, 1956**

In anticipation of the November 15 premiere of *Love Me Tender*, a 40-foot cut-out figure of Elvis was unveiled on the marquee of the Paramount Theater in New York's Times Square. A crowd of 1,000 squealing fans mobbed the theater when the doors were opened on the day of the premiere, some of them having stood in line all of the previous night.

Above: **Gladys and Vernon Presley, 1956**

For Elvis' proud parents, even the daily mail delivery had changed forever. Here they pose for a photograph with just one day's typical stack of gifts from fans all over the world.

Left: **A teenage fan, Atlantic City, 1957**

Dream on. Across the world, teenage fans' bedrooms were soon covered in images of the undisputed King of Rock'n'Roll.

Above: **Sun Studios, Memphis, December 4, 1956**
Elvis at Sun Studios, jamming with (standing left to right) Jerry Lee Lewis, Carl Perkins, and Johnny Cash. It became known as the Million Dollar Quartet, although Cash never sang on any of the songs preserved on tape.

Right: **With George Klein, 1956**
George Klein was an old high school friend of Elvis who became a prominent Memphis disc jockey. Elvis occasionally dropped in for a visit.

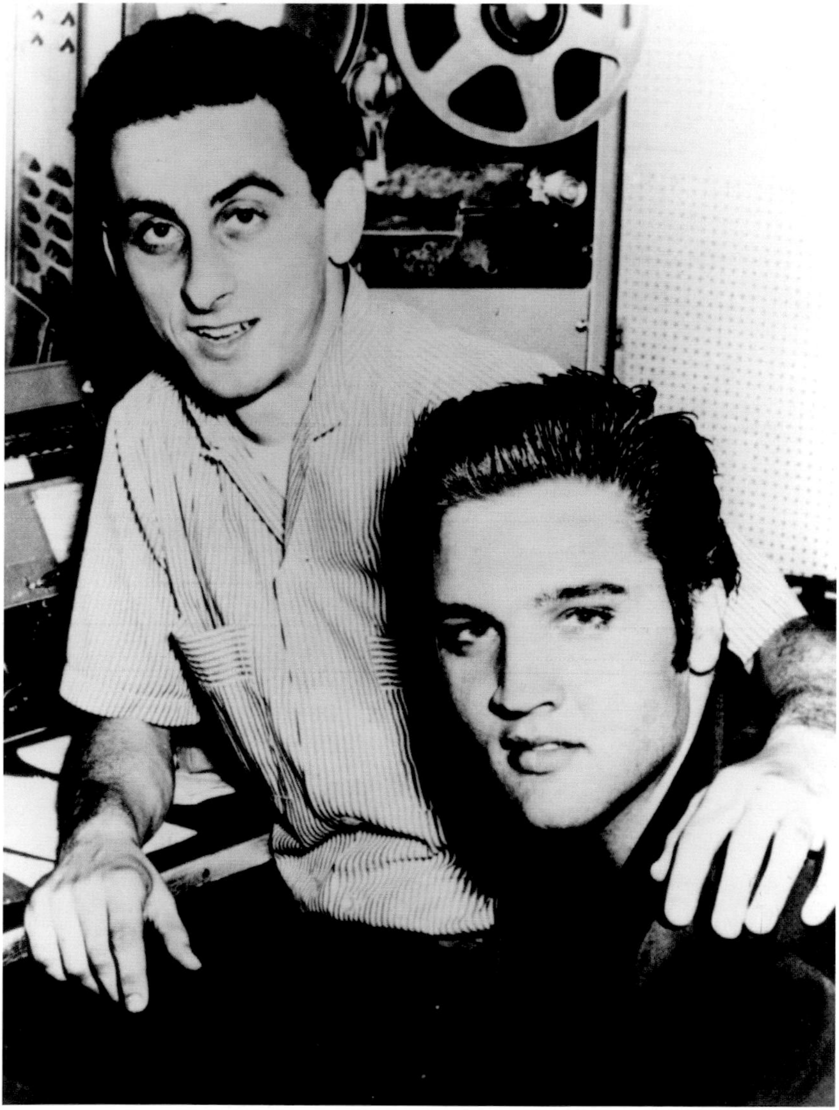

Above: **Gladys, Elvis, and Vernon Presley, 21–22 February, 1957**

Elvis with his parents on the set of his second film, *Loving You.*

Elvis Presley's second screen appearance ... exposes the singer to the kind of thing he does best, i.e. shout out his rhythms, bang away at his guitar and perform the strange, knee-bending, hip-swinging contortions that are his trademark.

Variety, reviewing Loving You, July 1957

Loving You

The story of a young country singer whose rise to fame is not without its ups and downs, and with plenty of excuses for Elvis to break into song.

Studio: Paramount
Released: July 1957
Producer: Hal B. Wallis
Director: Hal Kanter
Format: Technicolor/Vistavision
Leads: Elvis Presley, Lizabeth Scott, Wendell Corey

Right: **Still from Loving You, February 1957**

Actress Dolores Hart in a scene from Elvis' second movie, in which we can also see band members including drummer D.J. Fontana (far left) and guitarist Scotty Moore (far right).

Above: **Still from Loving You, February 1957**

Unlike his role in *Love Me Tender*, Elvis was really in character for *Loving You*, playing a young country singer, Deke Rivers, on the way up.

Below: **Strand Theater, Memphis, July 9, 1957**

The premiere of *Loving You*, not attended by Elvis, was held in the Strand movie theater in Memphis, accompanied by the inevitable screams of adoring fans.

Above: **Venetia Stevenson, August 8, 1957**

Another Hollywood date was actress Venetia Stevenson, daughter of actress, Anna Lee and director Robert Stevenson. During a three-day visit to Memphis, Elvis took her to a private screening of *Loving You* at the Strand Theater.

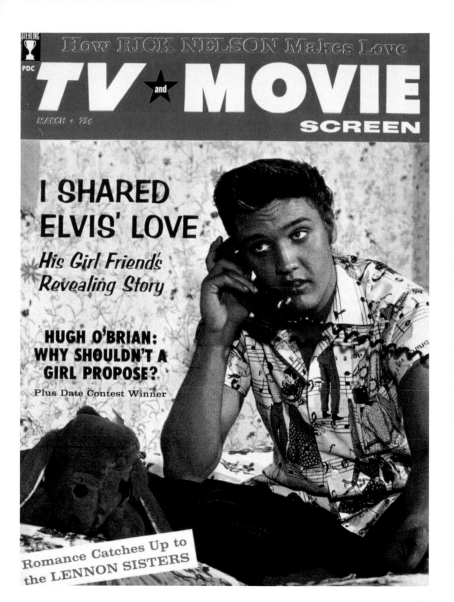

How RICK NELSON Makes Love

TV and MOVIE
SCREEN

MARCH • 25¢

I SHARED ELVIS' LOVE
His Girl Friend's Revealing Story

HUGH O'BRIAN: WHY SHOULDN'T A GIRL PROPOSE?

Plus Date Contest Winner

Romance Catches Up to the LENNON SISTERS

Left: **The gold lamé suit, March 1957**

In March 1957, the Colonel had the famous gold lamé suit made for Elvis by Nudie Cohen, who specialized in colorful outfits for country music stars. The full suit, which Elvis only wore a few times on tour, eventually appeared on the cover of his 1959 "greatest hits" album, *50,000,000 Elvis Fans Can't Be Wrong.*

Right: **On stage, April 1957**

For the majority of his March–April tour in 1957, Elvis only wore the gold jacket with black trousers, after the gold on the pants began flaking off when he dropped to his knees.

Graceland

As Elvis's fame grew, so did the need for a larger home. After his initial success, the Presleys rented a single family home. But by the time of Hollywood, Elvis bought a suburban brick home in a quiet neighborhood. Fans followed the Presleys, and the neighbors on Audubon Drive seemed pleased by neither the teeming throngs who suddenly became a fixture nor by Gladys' chicken coop. These affluent neighbors made noises about buying the Presleys out, to which Elvis threw back an offer to buy *them* out. But it was clear that the family needed a new place to live—grander, more private, more suited to the reputation of an international star. They needed Graceland.

Elvis loved the place as soon as he saw it. Ignoring Vernon's advice, he bought the home at the full asking price, and renovations commenced immediately. There were two things Elvis was adamant about—a real soda fountain, and the most beautiful bedroom in Memphis for his mother. Taking Sam Phillips' new home as a model, he planned to paint his bedroom in "the darkest blue there is … I probably will have a black bedroom suite, trimmed in white leather, with a white [llama] rug [like Sam's]." His initial color scheme for the living and dining rooms—purple and gold—were toned down a notch by Gladys. Author Elaine Dundy tells a story which illustrates Elvis' baroque and precipitous tastes: "There is also a story … that Vernon came to him one day saying, 'I just went by Donald's Furniture Store and they've got the ugliest furniture I've ever seen in my life.' After he described it, Elvis said 'Good! That sounds like me.' At Donald's it took Elvis just thirty minutes to furnish his den."

Gladys got the bedroom of her dreams, and spent much of her time there. Neighbors from East Tupelo, the Lauderdale Courts—even Audubon Drive—described Gladys as a gregarious

and generous neighbor. At Graceland, she would initially interact with the fans, even inviting some of them in. But as Elvis' fame grew, her world shrank. Afraid for her son's well-being, physically isolated by the 18 acres that surrounded Graceland, prevented from performing household chores by a well-meaning son and a trained staff, Gladys became increasingly depressed and withdrawn. Friends and family noted her ill health and sad demeanor, but, in the end, nothing could save her. She died at forty-six, twenty-two years and two days before her son's depression and isolation would bring him home to her.

Left and above: **Graceland, Highway 51, June 1958**

Elvis purchased the new family home in the Memphis suburb of Whitehaven for $102,500 in March 1957.

Previous page: **Elvis at the gates, April 26, 1957**

Soon after purchasing Graceland, Elvis commissioned iron gates with a distinctive music design. They were installed on April 22 at the bottom of the long drive to Graceland. Several days later, Elvis proudly posed before them.

 Jailhouse Rock

In what was essentially a drama, Elvis plays Vince Everett, a singing truck driver in trouble with the law.

Studio: **MGM**
Released: **November 1957**
Producer: **Pandro S. Berman**
Director: **Richard Thorpe**
Format: **Monochrome/Cinemascope**
Leads: **Elvis Presley, Judy Tyler,**
　　　Mickey Shaughnessy

Left: **Still from Jailhouse Rock,
May 13–14, 1957**

The "prison" dance sequence in *Jailhouse Rock*, which was choreographed by Alex Romero, has become one of the key items in Elvis iconography.

This time most of his singing can actually be understood. And in two numbers, "Treat Me Nice" and the title song, done as a convict jamboree, Elvis breaks loose with his St. Vitus specialty. Ten to one, next time he'll make it—finally getting those kneecaps turned inside out and cracking them together like coconuts. Never say die, El.

New York Times, on Jailhouse Rock

Above: **Still from Jailhouse Rock, May–June 1957**

Co-star Mickey Shaughnessy in the role of Elvis' cellmate, a former country singer, who befriends the young Vince Everett, even lending him his guitar.

Jerry Leiber and Mike Stoller

If Elvis Presley was the king of rock and roll, the songwriting team of Leiber and Stoller built the throne. Both born in 1933, they met in Los Angeles in 1950 and formed a partnership that would produce some of the most dynamic hits of rock and roll.

Leiber was raised on the edge of Baltimore's black ghetto, while Stoller, born in Belle Harbor, New York, learned the blues and boogie woogie from the black kids at summer camp. Stoller, a classically trained musician with a passion for R&B and the blues, wrote the music, while Leiber provided artful, witty lyrics.

In 1953, Big Mama Thornton recorded their "Hound Dog," creating an R&B hit that Elvis Presley picked up on. Three years later he released it (with Otis Blackwell's "Don't Be Cruel" on the flip side). It hit #1 and stayed there for eleven weeks; it would take 36 years for another single to maintain that status for that long.

The Jewish boys composing black music found a compadre in the white kid singing it. Elvis recorded more than 20 Leiber and Stoller tunes, including "Bossa Nova Baby," "She's Not You," and "Santa Claus is Back in Town." They wrote songs for him, and worked closely on the films *Loving You* and *Jailhouse Rock*. More accurately described as "pop auteurs," Leiber and Stoller arranged and produced their material. "We don't write songs. We write records," stated the duo. Though their masterful touch brought Elvis undoubted success, their influence still made Parker uneasy.

This relationship ended in 1958. Their presence was requested by Elvis at a January recording session for *King Creole*. Leiber, however, was in the emergency ward with pneumonia and missed the calls. The Colonel became increasingly infuriated and sent Leiber a "contract" which consisted of a blank piece of paper with his signature at the bottom, and a line for them to sign. "We'll fill in

Above: **With Leiber and Stoller, April–May 1957**
Elvis studies the sheet music for "Jailhouse Rock" with the song's two writers Leiber and Stoller, during the soundtrack recording for the movie of the same name.

the details later," the Colonel stated. The songwriters had finally had enough. "We never worked with him again. That was it."

But it wasn't the end of hits for Leiber and Stoller. More than 200 of their songs were recorded in the 1950s and 1960s, titles often recorded multiple times by various artists. The Coasters (née the Robins) had twenty-four chart hits alone. They produced artists as diverse as T-Bone Walker, Perry Como, and in the 1970s, Stealer's Wheel ("Stuck In The Middle With You"). In 1995, their musical review *Smokey Joe's Café* opened on Broadway.

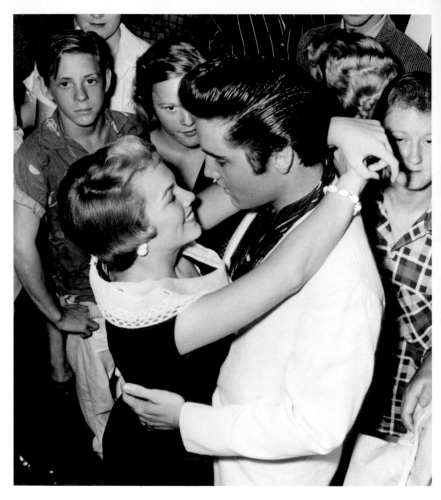

Above: **With Anita Wood, Memphis, August 28, 1957**

Elvis had been dating Memphis beauty queen Anita Wood since early July 1957. Here they part company at the railroad station—Elvis leaving to tour, Anita for the finals of a Hollywood Star Hunt contest (which she went on to win).

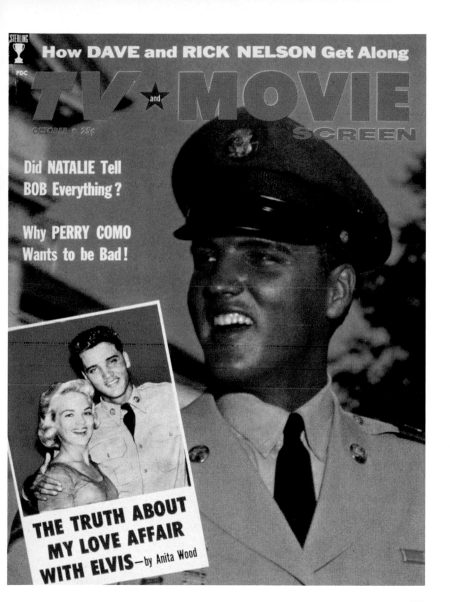

TV and MOVIE SCREEN
STERLING
PDC

OCTOBER • 25¢

Did NATALIE Tell
BOB Everything?

Why PERRY COMO
Wants to be Bad!

THE TRUTH ABOUT
MY LOVE AFFAIR
WITH ELVIS—by Anita Wood

The part gives him scope to stop behaving like an electrocuted baboon and to act like a human being, which he does with a new skill, a new restraint, and a new charm.

News Chronicle, July 1958

 King Creole

Based on the Harold Robbins novel *A Stone For Danny Fisher*, this was a melodrama in which Elvis played a New Orleans youngster who gets mixed up in local nightclubs, the gangsters that run them, and—inevitably—their girls.

Studio: Paramount
Released: July 1958
Producer: Hal B. Wallis

Director: Michael Curtiz
Format: Monochrome
Leads: Elvis Presley, Carolyn Jones, Walter Matthau, Dolores Hart

Above and right: **Publicity shots, King Creole, 1958**

Publicity shots promoting *King Creole*, including Elvis with (clockwise) female co-stars Dolores Hart, Jan Shepard, Liliane Montevecchi, and Carolyn Jones.

Above: **Backstage at the Grand Ole Opry, Nashville, December 21, 1957**

In Nashville to deliver Tom Parker's Christmas present, at the end of 1957 Elvis dropped in to the Grand Ole Opry to make a guest non-singing appearance. Here he poses with country stars (left to right) Ferlin Husky, Faron Young and Hawkshaw Hawkins, and D.J.-promoter-booking agent Tom Perryman.

Above: **Backstage at the Grand Ole Opry, Nashville, December 21, 1957**

Also at the Opry date was Elvis' old Sun label-mate Johnny Cash. Prior to visiting the show, Elvis decided he needed something to wear, and was taken to a local clothing store by Jordanaire Gordon Stoker where he selected a smart tuxedo, which he binned immediately afterwards!

The army can do anything it wants with me. Millions of other guys have been drafted, and I don't want to be different to anyone else.

Right: **Army induction, Memphis, January 4, 1957**
Early in 1957 Elvis took his pre-induction written examination for the U.S. Army, and a physical at the Kennedy Veterans' Hospital in Memphis. He was accompanied by Dottie Harmony, a Las Vegas dancer he was dating.

Elvis arrived on the scene when the young needed a romantic image. He filled the bill and on top of that, he can sing.

Marlene Dietrich

Right: **Graceland, December 20, 1957**
Elvis reading his notice from the Memphis Draft Board that he was to be conscripted for military service. He received it the first Christmas the Presley family spent at their new home. After he made a formal request for a deferment in order to complete his next film, scheduled for early in the new year, the Board agreed to defer his entry until March, 1958.

Previous page: **Army Induction Center, March 24, 1958**

Elvis reported to the Memphis Draft Board at 198 South Main Street with his parents and friends. Next to Elvis sits his mother, Judy Spreckels (center), girlfriend Anita Wood (second right), and Bonnie Underwood (far right).

Above and right: **Kennedy Veterans Memorial Hospital, March 24, 1958**

After being sworn in, the thirteen new recruits were bussed to the hospital where they underwent a medical exam, after which Elvis said goodbye to his forlorn-looking parents. (Right) Private Elvis Presley—now soldier number 53 310 761—waves farewell as he boards the bus to take him and the rest of the group to Fort Chaffee, Arkansas.

I had to get used to a certain way of life. It's hard for anybody to adjust to the Army, and maybe it was harder for me than for most. But I was determined to adjust, because any other way I would only have hurt myself.

Right: **Fort Chaffee, Arkansas, March 25, 1958**

Induction continued at Fort Chaffee, accompanied by over fifty journalists and photographers, making Elvis' haircut probably the most publicized in U.S. Army history.

Following page: **Fort Chaffee, Arkansas, March 25, 1958**

The Colonel was clearly in his element. Here he chats to two executives from RCA Records while, dressed in fatigues in the background, Elvis selects his army clothing. It was a long way from Lansky's.

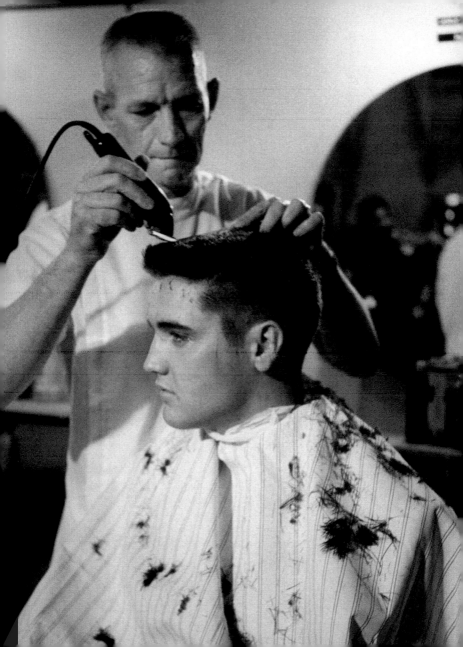

It may surprise you, but I am a Presley fan. Elvis recently saw my folks in California and told them he was a fan of mine, that I had been an inspiration to him... What that boy has done is phenomenal. He has busted many of the disc sales records I held, in little over a year.

Mario Lanza

Right: **Fort Hood, Texas, March 28, 1958**

While at Fort Chaffee, Elvis was assigned to the Second Armored Division stationed at Fort Hood in Texas, where he arrives complete with kit bag.

Left: **Memphis, June 4, 1958**

After completing his basic training, Elvis enjoyed a furlough at home. He took his parents to a preview of *King Creole*.

Above: **Vernon and Elvis, August 14, 1958**

After months of increasing ill health, Elvis' mother Gladys died from an undiagnosed liver complaint. He and his father were completely distraught, his cousin Harold Loyd recalling years later that Elvis was "in pitiful shape. His eyes were all swollen and red."

He sat on his butt in the snow like the rest of us and ate the same crummy food we did. He was a real Joe.

an army buddy

Right: **Friedberg, West Germany, 1958**

On base, Elvis enjoyed no more privileges than any other "G.I. Joe." Later, because of his dependents (his father and grandmother) he was allowed, in accordance with regulations, to live off base.

Following page: **Frankfurt, October 23, 1958**

When the other original rock'n'roll idol, Bill Haley, was appearing in Frankfurt, Elvis caught his concert and visited him backstage in full Army uniform.

Above: **Frankfurt, December 21, 1958**

A model presents Elvis with the keys to a sports car he has leased. The BMW 507 formerly belonged to the German auto racer Hans Stuck, and Elvis reportedly had the racing motor exchanged for a "tamer" engine.

He was the roughest, toughest, most gung-ho soldier I ever had under my command—to this day, and I mean that, despite thousands of soldiers I've been involved with. He was a born fighter. Elvis took no prisoners.

**Colonel William J. Taylor Jr.,
Elvis' former commanding officer**

Right: **Karate in Paris, January 1960**

Elvis made two trips to Paris on Army leave. On the second trip in January 1960 he attended five karate classes given by Tetsuji Murakami (in the picture with Elvis), a Japanese teacher of the shotokan technique.

Romance in Germany

Female companionship came quickly, but all infatuations (if not dalliances) subsided when Elvis met Priscilla Beaulieu, a fourteen-year-old beauty who caught his eye. A friend assured her mother and stepfather, an Air Force Captain, of Elvis' good intentions, then brought Priscilla to Elvis. She was immediately smitten and somewhat awed. Despite her extreme youth, or perhaps because of it, Elvis quickly fell under the almost-silent girl's spell, not even daunted by the fact that she had yet to finish ninth grade. Soon after, Elvis traveled to her house, disarmingly declaring his affection and respect for Priscilla. Reassured, Priscilla's parents allowed her to visit the twenty-five-year-old singer/soldier almost nightly.

There was another romance brewing in the Presley household, and this one was much less pleasing to Elvis. Vernon Presley, devoted to Gladys while she was alive, became enamored of Dee Stanley, the pretty blonde wife of Sergeant Bill Stanley and the mother of three boys. Elvis distrusted Dee and her intentions, and was insulted that Vernon could replace Gladys so quickly. Nonetheless, Dee, who had been having troubles with her hard-drinking husband long before Vernon showed up, soon left Germany for West Virginia. Vernon followed, trying unsuccessfully to avoid a hungry press. By July 3, 1960, Dee and Vernon would marry, moving themselves and Dee's three sons into Graceland after the honeymoon.

Above: **Priscilla Beaulieu, March 1960**

Priscilla had only begun dating Elvis six weeks before his departure from Germany. Here, at her family's home in Wiesbaden, she gazes at a picture of Elvis as she writes him a letter.

Above: **Bad Nauheim, March 2, 1960**

Elvis's grandmother Minnie Mae being led to a car by Priscilla Beaulieu, as she leaves the house at 14 Goethestrasse, Bad Nauheim, to return to the USA.

Left: **Fort Dix, NJ, March 3, 1960**

Elvis arrives in the middle of a snowstorm at McGuire Air Force Base near Fort Dix, New Jersey for a couple of days, prior to his release from his Army service.

Left: **Elvis and Priscilla,
March 2, 1960**

Elvis chats to fans through
the window of his car as
he and Priscilla drive to
the Rhine-Main air base
for his flight home. *Life*
magazine described the
tearful girlfriend as "The
Girl He Left Behind."

Movieland

chapter 4

Off the road 1960–1968

Although Elvis hadn't seen any action in Europe, there was carnage at RCA. The Colonel had insisted there be no new recordings while Elvis was in the army, shrewdly ensuring that, when he returned, RCA would be desperate for material. Desperate—and vulnerable to whatever demands Parker wished to impose upon the record company.

The Colonel was also working the Hollywood front. Hal Wallis, after a series of battles with Parker, got what he wanted—Elvis in a movie. The Colonel also got what he wanted—$175,000, plus bonuses and profit participation. In addition, 20th Century Fox exercised its option for two more Elvis pictures that same year. From the three films alone, the twenty-five-year-old would be guaranteed income of over half-a-million dollars in 1960. In addition, MGM was at the door waiting to negotiate a deal. Welcome home, soldier!

There was little time to spend at Graceland. After the obligatory press conference, he called Memphis girlfriend Anita Wood, reunited with his old friends, and visited his mother's room, untouched—by his orders—since her death. But he was due in Nashville to record for an almost-frantic RCA. Scotty Moore, D.J. Fontana and The Jordanaires were on hand, as were Nashville heavies like pianist Floyd Cramer and guitarist Hank Garland. Just as at Graceland, there was the eerie sense of never having left, and yet, there was something missing. They recorded his new single "Stuck on You" (flip side: "Fame and Fortune"), but with the exception of "A Mess of Blues," nothing rose above the catchy and formulaic. The labels were printed before the session, and RCA pressed 1.4 million advance orders with the title, "Elvis' 1st New Recording For His 50,000,000 Fans All Over the World."

His first big engagement was on a Frank Sinatra television

special. Sinatra, who came from a background remarkably similar to Elvis', had previously been less than charitable to Presley and his music. But the public's continued adoration for Elvis had apparently caused Sinatra to put his baleful attitude behind him.

Then Elvis was back in Nashville to finish recording the upcoming album *Elvis is Back*, which included a version of Peggy Lee's hit "Fever," "The Girl Of My Best Friend," and the old Johnnie Ray potboiler "Such A Night." The standout track was his rendition of Lowell Fulson's "Reconsider Baby," which features the Elvis magnetism—a charisma that Hollywood would soon thoroughly mis-market.

His first effort back in Hollywood was accurately titled *G.I. Blues*. Everything was so perfectly planned, Elvis almost didn't have to show up. And, in a way, he didn't. His first session at the RCA studio in Hollywood foretold his future—the songs were largely bland and uninspiring. Writers and producers Leiber and Stoller, banished by Parker, were greatly missed. The film was no better. Elvis became increasingly humiliated and resentful at being denied the opportunity to grapple with a real part.

When he was off duty, however, he stayed busy. He began dating Sandy Ferra, a sixteen-year-old attending the Hollywood Professional School; flew in Memphian Bonnie Bunkley, a Priscilla lookalike, for a week; dallied with co-star Juliet Prowse (who was dating Frank Sinatra at the time); kept Anita Wood on ice back home; and checked in on that pretty little girl in Germany. Parties with Sammy Davis, Jr. and Bobby Darin alternated with raucous nights at the Beverly Wilshire Hotel.

Popular music, at least in recording sessions, seemed to have lost its patina. But one October night in Nashville, a week before his next picture was to begin, music regained its shine. Elvis had longed for a chance to record the music of his youth—gospel. With Chet Atkins and The Jordanaires, "His Hand in Mine" was recorded in one night, a session that stretched until 8 a.m. the following morning. "Crying in the Chapel," "He Knows Just What I Need," and "Surrender" were among the fourteen sides recorded. Inspired by his idol Jake Hess of The Statesmen, Elvis was nothing less than masterful.

Elvis' generous nature was well-known among friends and family, and in November 1960 he announced that his first live appearance since the army would be a charity concert at Ellis Auditorium in Memphis. The fundraiser, slated for February, would benefit twenty-six local charities, including the Elvis Youth Center in Tupelo. The concert raised over $50,000, and the state legislature officially commended Elvis as "one of Memphis' most outstanding citizens." In December, Colonel Parker learned that the U.S.S. Arizona memorial to the Pearl Harbor soldiers was $50,000 short of its goal, and he announced that Elvis would come to Hawaii to help raise the completion funds. He raised over $62,000 in Hawaii, and, for the second time in a month, the ghost of pre-Army Elvis hovered close. Inexplicably, it would be another eight years before he performed live.

Instead, Elvis would make twenty-five more pictures in the 1960s, each one more vapid and spiritless than the previous. Regardless of which studio produced the film, each followed the directive given to Paramount's script writer Allan Weiss: "I was asked to create a believable framework for twelve songs and lots of girls." On the sets, Elvis was invariably known for his punctuality, professionalism, and courtesy to his fellow actors and crew members.

But off the set, Elvis seemed bored and unhappy. He had always had a bad temper, cajoled and indulged by an adoring mother. But now, surrounded by friends who had become employees, his temper had fired into something far worse. During one party, he grabbed actress Christina Crawford by the hair and dragged her around his living room; another night he threw a pool cue at a young lady during an argument. And his companions were increasingly wary and sometimes resentful of his creeping paranoia: his surveillance of possible dissension in the ranks, his condition that he be the center of attention each time, every time.

It seemed as if nothing would ever be different: each movie role would be stupider; each possession would be grander; each night would be longer. It was time for a change—and her name was Priscilla.

Priscilla's plane touched down in Los Angeles in June, 1962. Elvis spent the next two weeks escorting the diffident teenager—on sightseeing tours, to shows, on shopping sprees. When she returned home in July, her parents were appalled at her Elvisized hair and make-up. But Priscilla was defiant; Elvis was her future.

At Christmas, Priscilla was again whisked to America to visit her determined suitor. Their two passionate, if technically chaste, weeks whirled by, the brevity heightened by Priscilla's two-day coma, courtesy of some "nerve" pills prescribed by Dr. Elvis. Upon Priscilla's return home, she gave her parents an ultimatum: She would return to Elvis or she would give her parents an endless seminar on the behavior of a furious teenager. The Beaulieus never had a chance. By March, Captain Beaulieu and his daughter flew to Los Angeles where Elvis was filming his latest tour de force, *Fun In Acapulco.* The deal was sealed. Priscilla moved to Memphis, and enrolled in the dual life of a Catholic high school student and Elvis Presley's best-kept secret.

Priscilla graduated in May of 1963. Afterwards, Elvis and Priscilla stayed in his bedroom for three weeks, ordering up food, watching old movies, having pillow fights. Their sexual relationship was passionate and diverse, but always stopped short of intercourse, as Elvis wanted: "Don't let's get carried away, baby. Let me decide when it should happen. It's a very sacred thing to me." The world was a million miles away, on the other side of the blackout drapes and tinfoil that habitually covered Elvis' bedroom windows.

Time and Hollywood waited for no man, not even Elvis. By July he was back for MGM's *Viva Las Vegas.* His sense of obligation must have lessened when he met his co-star, Ann-Margret. Within two weeks, the press was broadcasting their romance. His outrage at the news of their alleged engagement was nothing to Priscilla's reaction. He confessed the details of the relationship, swore his allegiance to Priscilla and got her out of town after promising to break all ties with Ann.

Furious with the high production costs and long shooting time of *Viva Las Vegas,* Colonel Parker pursued producer Sam Katzman, who was legendary for his strict adherence to the bottom line. When they met, the chemistry that had sizzled between Elvis and Ann-Margret paled; these two were soul mates. Under their aegis, *Kissin' Cousins* began production in October of 1963. The film wrapped in a record seventeen days.

Paramount's *Roustabout* was next on the agenda, a carnival film. Having viewed *Viva Las Vegas*, producer Hal Wallis wrote to the Colonel that Elvis was overweight; he seemed "soft" and "jowly," and his hair was "atrocious." But less attention was given to the soundtrack and the script, which were miserable.

Elvis publicly and repeatedly expressed his sense of betrayal at the hands of Wallis and of the Colonel. But he was twenty-nine years old. He was in the 90 percent tax bracket. Many people depended on him. And he was lost.

In March of 1965, a search for inner peace via a new-found "guru," Larry Geller, helped Elvis through the miseries of yet another Sam Katzman production. *Harum Scarum* was a project that initially excited Elvis. He was delighted by the costumes, which were intended to give Elvis an appeal reminiscent of

Rudolph Valentino—one of Elvis' idols. But the film, directed by Gene Nelson, was quickly exposed for the shabby enterprise that it was. On the last day of filming *Harum*, Elvis gave Nelson an autographed picture with the hopeful inscription, "Some day we'll do it right."

That day was not on his next film, *Frankie and Johnny*, which began production almost immediately. The only real interest Elvis showed was in his co-star Donna Douglas, though it was platonic. Douglas (Ellie Mae of *The Beverly Hillbillies*) was a fellow member of the Self-Realization Fellowship, a religious organization founded by Paramahansa Yogananda, author of the spiritual classic *Autobiography of a Yogi.* He was thrilled to have a fellow path-seeker on the set; together they shared books and meditated.

Another rewarding moment came when his song "Crying in the Chapel," recorded five years earlier, was released and became his first top ten hit since 1962. The song reached number one on the British charts, a first for Elvis since the Fab Four had descended on the world. Elvis had publicly welcomed the British Invasion, saying there was room in the business for everyone. Nevertheless, Elvis, stuck on a treadmill of schlocky movies and vapid soundtracks, was gratified to beat The Beatles.

The Colonel had kept his eyes on the Liverpool group since their appearance on *The Ed Sullivan Show*, and persuaded Elvis that a meeting between the King and the Fab Four was great publicity. At 10 p.m., on August 27 1965 The Beatles and their manager Brian Epstein arrived at Elvis' California home. The whole entourage was there, spouses and girlfriends as well; everyone was thrilled at the prospect of meeting The Beatles— except Elvis. As the light of the soundless TV lit up his unimpressed visage, Elvis fingered his bass to the tune playing on his jukebox, Charlie Rich's "Mohair Sam." No one was impressed; Elvis was later described by Beatles' press officer as "a boring old fart."

However, when one of Elvis' friends stopped by The Beatles' house over the weekend (Elvis had declined the invite), John Lennon declared that without Elvis, "I would have been nothing." Elvis smiled when he heard that.

Back in Memphis for the first time in seven months, Elvis was able to enjoy the latest addition to Graceland—the Meditation Garden. Inspired by the Self-Realization Park in California, he wanted Graceland to have "some place that's really pretty and peaceful where I could think and be by myself." With Italian marble statues, stained glass windows from Spain, brick from Mexico, and a fountain that featured fourteen sprays and an underwater light formation, the Garden took a year and $21,000 to complete. When Elvis saw it completed, he had tears in his eyes. When Vernon saw the bill, he did too.

The success of "Crying in the Chapel" had been an inspiration, and Elvis began preparing a new, non-soundtrack album. There was a sense that Elvis was back. *How Great Thou Art* came out in February 1967. Of all his albums, Elvis was proudest of this one, which became his first Grammy-winner, taking the year's Best Sacred Performance.

Back in Memphis after the predictably tepid release of the movie *Spinout,* Elvis made his usual generous donation—$105,000—to local charities, but he didn't really feel the Christmas spirit until Priscilla got her gift—a horse. Elvis quickly bought himself a Golden Palomino named Rising Sun and horses for all the guys. The passion for horses quickly outstripped the space at Graceland. For a half-a-million dollars, Elvis bought a ranch in Mississippi, named it the Flying Circle G in his mother's memory, and collected all the accoutrements necessary for a gentleman rancher. In Hollywood he was little more than chattel, but here in Mississippi, damn it, he owned the world.

At the ranch, he was having so much fun that he didn't want

to pay the piper. When it came time to make *Clambake*, he delayed his return. Furious, the Colonel demanded that he present a doctor's note to justify holding up production. That weekend, his doctor's partner was on call, Dr. George Nichopoulos. He readily agreed to treat Elvis's "saddle sores," but when he got there, the real reason for his visit was revealed; would the good doctor write a note to Hollywood, excusing Elvis from school? He consented. Elvis liked "Dr. Nick," a mild-mannered man whose shock of white hair belied his 39 years and athletic physique. It was probable that he also enjoyed the good doctor's quick accession to his demands. Dr. Nick would soon be an invaluable addition to Elvis's entourage.

Easy Come, Easy Go flopped at the box office, and the soundtrack sales tanked. *Double Trouble* opened a few weeks later and did even worse. If the public was tiring of the formula, Elvis was about to change the recipe: under a veil of secrecy, Priscilla and Elvis and a small group of friends were flown to Las Vegas on two private jets, one belonging to Frank Sinatra. On May 1, 1967 Elvis Presley and Priscilla Beaulieu were wed at a civil ceremony that lasted eight minutes; the press conference that immediately followed lasted longer.

After the newlyweds retreated to the Flying Circle G ranch, Priscilla returned with him to Hollywood, and in July Elvis announced that she was pregnant: "This is the greatest thing that ever happened to me."

On February 1,1968, Lisa Marie Presley was born, with the full head of brunette hair that both parents had dreamed of. "She's a little miracle," proclaimed Elvis, who picked up his daughter so often that Priscilla had to put an end to the fussing. But Elvis' elation didn't extend to his marriage. He had never been able to sleep with women who had borne children, and Priscilla, to her mortification, was now relegated to the Madonna sphere.

The next soundtrack session was so pitiful that Elvis rejected all RCA's offerings, displaying a hitherto hidden but profound resentment. It was, for Elvis, one of the many instances of the Colonel's interference. His films, his songs, his career was in a stranglehold. Sales were way down, as were his hopes of being taken seriously as an actor or a musician.

The Colonel, realizing that the movie offers were running dry, headed for television. NBC agreed to finance a motion picture for Elvis, and they would get Elvis for a Christmas special—his first television appearance in eight years.

He applied himself like he hadn't in a long time, and *Singer Presents Elvis* became ever known as "the Comback." After the success of the Christmas TV show, the Colonel worked quickly. He contacted the International Hotel in Vegas and a deal was struck. For four weeks in July, seven nights a week, Elvis would headline two shows a night. The salary was $100,000 per week.

In January of 1969, Christmas kept coming. Elvis was scheduled to record at RCA in Nashville, but he decided to stay home. The past eighteen months had seen an unprecedented 164 hits come out of a little studio in North Memphis called American Sound Studio, and the reason was producer Chips Moman, who had been involved in the foundation of the ground-breaking Stax Studio. He gathered the best and the brightest musicians Memphis had to offer, including the guitarist Reggie Young, bassist and producer Tommy Cogbill, bass player Mike Leech, drummer Gene Chrisman, and Bobby Emmons and Bobby Wood on organ. Together they were making music history.

When Moman got word that Elvis wanted to record, he was keen, though the studio musicians were initially reluctant. But when he entered the studio on January 13, 1969, Elvis quickly shed all of the layers that success had enshrouded him in, moving through nine takes of "Long Black Limousine" with a bad cold, but increasing emotion. Elvis packed the song with the kind of naked feeling that his best performances evoked. He left the sessions with "Suspicious Minds" and "In the Ghetto." He'd hesitated to record the latter because of its overt political slant, but "In the Ghetto" hit the charts two weeks after it was shipped out, reaching number three on June 14, giving Elvis his first Top Ten hit and gold record since 1965. The album *Elvis in Memphis* was released in June of 1969. The sales weren't extraordinary, but the album was, as *Rolling Stone* magazine stated: "flatly and unequivocally the equal of anything he has ever done." He was ready to return to the stage.

There is something magical about watching a man who has lost himself find his way back home... He sang with the kind of power people no longer expect from rock'n'roll singers.

Jon Landau (review of '68 Comeback)

Left: **Fort Dix, New Jersey, March 3, 1960**

On his arrival at Fort Dix before his final discharge, the Army held a press conference and a welcome party that included Colonel Tom Parker, RCA representatives, and singer Nancy Sinatra. Here, Elvis is greeted by Nancy Sinatra, and a gift from her father, Frank—a pair of formal lace-fronted shirts.

Rock'n'roll is sung, played, and written for the most part by cretinous goons and by means of its almost imbecilic reiteration, and sly, lewd, in plain fact, dirty lyrics ... it manages to be the martial music of every sideburned delinquent on the face of the earth... (It) is the most brutal, ugly, desperate, vicious form of expression it has been my misfortune to hear.

Frank Sinatra, 1958

Right: **The Frank Sinatra Show, March 26, 1960**
Despite his comments about rock'n'roll just a couple of years earlier, Frank Sinatra featured Elvis on his TV special, billed as "Frank Sinatra's Welcome Home Party for Elvis Presley." Recorded on March 26, the show was broadcast on May 12.

Man, I got butterflies, I've been waiting for this day for two long years.

Left: **The Frank Sinatra Show, March 26, 1960**

The Sinatra show was taped in Miami. Elvis, impeccably groomed and elegantly attired, was joined by "Rat Pack" members Sammy Davis Jr., Peter Lawford and Joey Bishop—plus Nancy Sinatra, seen here with Elvis and her father, Frank. Elvis sang "Fame and Fortune" and "Stuck on You," and closed the show by joining 'Ole Blue Eyes in a duet, a rendition of Frank's "Witchcraft" which trumped Sinatra's conspicuously unhip treatment of "Love Me Tender."

G.I. Blues

Clearly cashing in on Elvis' much-publicized time in the US Army, the plot concerns three Army buddies who form a rock'n'roll band while stationed in Germany—Elvis' character Tulsa McLean gets involved with cabaret star, Lili, played by Juliet Prowse.

Studio: Paramount
Released: November, 1960
Producer: Hal B. Wallis
Director: Norman Taurog
Format: Technicolor
Leads: Elvis Presley, Juliet Prowse

Right: **Poster, G.I. Blues, November 1960**

G.I. Blues could be seen as a public relations exercise, selling post-Army Elvis as a regular guy who was good with kids (and puppets), and thereby deftly guiding families to go to his films and to buy his records. And they did—the film was a hit, and the soundtrack album far outsold the vastly superior *Elvis is Back*, released earlier in the year.

ALLIS JULIET PROWSE Co-starring Directed by NORMAN TAUROG
Written by EDMUND BELOIN and HENRY GARSON
A PARAMOUNT RELEASE   TECHNICOLOR®

Above: **Still from G.I. Blues, May–June 1960**

Elvis sings "Wooden Heart" to a puppet, one of the family-friendly scenes that characterized *G.I. Blues*.

Right: **Still from G.I. Blues, May–June 1960**

Elvis played opposite the song-and-dance actress Juliet Prowse in a plot that was as improbable as his stilted coiffure would be for a soldier.

Right: **RCA Studios, Hollywood, April 1960**

Elvis in the recording studio with The Jordanaires for the soundtrack work on *G.I. Blues*, which they recorded over two days at the end of April 1960.

Did you put a girdle on him? Did he have polio recently? There must be some explanation for all that lost motion ... Just who do you think buys 99.9 percent of his records? It ain't my mother.

Fan letter copied to Hal Wallis, the William Morris agency, RCA Records, Colonel Parker, and Paramount Pictures

Right: **California, November 1960**

While shooting *Wild in the Country*, Elvis posed for his official Christmas card for 1960, with Colonel Tom Parker dressed as Father Christmas.

Sincerely
Season's Greetings
Elvis
and
the Colonel

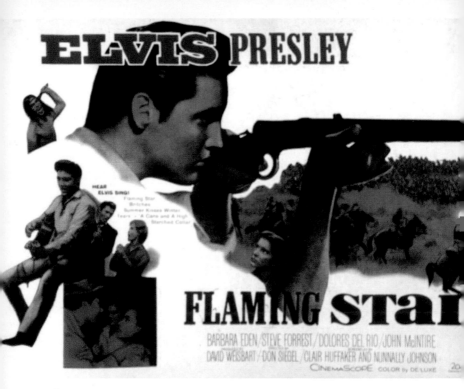

⭐ Flaming Star

Elvis plays a mixed-race Native American in a "serious" non-singing role, with just two songs, one over the credits. The plot addressed the clash of cultures faced by the hero's family. Elvis' part was originally planned for Marlon Brando.

Studio: 20th Century Fox
Released: December 1960
Producer: David Weisbart

Director: Don Siegel
Format: De Luxe color/Cinemascope
Leads: Elvis Presley, Steve Forrest, Dolores Del Rio, Barbara Eden

Above: **Publicity still, Flaming Star, 1960**

This publicity photograph for *Flaming Star* was to become part of Elvis iconography when adapted as a screen print entitled "Single Elvis" by pop artist Andy Warhol in 1963.

What really surprised me was the extraordinary talent of Elvis Presley. He took to this part as if he had been a dramatic actor all his life, with a particular feel for Odets' colorful and poetic dialogue.

Philip Dunne, director of "Wild In The Country"

Above: **Still from Wild In the Country, 1961**

Elvis and Hope Lange as Glenn Tyler and court psychiatrist Irene Speery, in whose care the rebellious country boy has been consigned.

Wild In The Country

Another drama, albeit with four songs, concerning a mistreated country boy (Elvis), who has the talent to become a successful writer, but lacks the confidence until he gets involved with an attractive psychiatrist.

Studio: 20th Century Fox
Released: June 1961
Producer: Jerry Wald

Director: Philip Dunne
Format: De Luxe color/Cinemascope
Leads: Elvis Presley, Hope Lange, Tuesday Weld

U.S.S. Arizona

A Nashville recording session was squeezed in before Elvis set off to Hawaii to start his newest movie and to prepare for the *U.S.S. Arizona* memorial fundraiser. The week before the concert, Parker blanketed the Hawaiian airwaves with Elvis singing spirituals; half of the radio stations donated the air-time. Elvis waived his fee. By the time he landed in Hawaii, there were 3,000 fans and seventy-five police officers to greet him. Minnie Pearl, who was escorting Elvis at the request of the Colonel, was horrified: "We got off the plane, girls were screaming … I'd never seen anything like it before … I thought … they were going to kill him."

In addition to Minnie Pearl, the concert included an orchestra featuring Polynesian-style music, piano music from Floyd Cramer, and singing from The Jordanaires. After intermission, the Admiral of the 14th Naval District read a telegram from the Secretary of the Navy: "The generosity and public spirited zeal with which you donate your services to the Arizona Memorial fund tonight are deeply appreciated by all of us in the Navy." To which the Admiral added, "He is a fine American."

This fine American, dazzling in a gold jacket, dark blue trousers, and a towering jet black coiffure, proceeded to rock the 4,800 Hawaiian fans. Crashing over the island like a tsunami, Elvis sang sixteen songs in just under an hour, including "Don't Be Cruel," "A Fool Such as I," "Surrender," and "Hound Dog." As in Memphis, Elvis was a consummate performer—elegant, controlled, but a powerhouse.

Right: **Honolulu airport, March 25, 1961**

Elvis arrives in Hawaii. It was to be the beginning of a love affair with the Pacific islands which continued throughout his career, starting with the filming of *Blue Hawaii* right after the Honolulu concert.

Elvis is a musical Messiah. For his fans, he had an animal magnetism that communicates itself more strongly than any entertainer I've seen or heard, an almost dictatorial control of the audience, which he wields over his disciples even when they can't hear the lyrics.

Honolulu Advertiser, March 27, 1961

Blue Hawaii

Against the backdrop of sun, sea, music, and bathing-suited girls, Elvis plays the rebellious son of a pineapple tycoon, returning from service in the Army to make his own way in life against the outcries of his conservative parents.

Studio: Paramount

Released: November 1961

Producer: Hal B. Wallis

Director: Norman Taurog

Format: Technicolor/Panavision

Leads: Elvis Presley, Joan Blackman, Angela Lansbury

Right: **Still from Blue Hawaii, April 1961**

The first of Elvis' "travelogue" films, which soon became a formula, *Blue Hawaii* grossed over $4 million at the box office, the soundtrack album selling over a million copies.

It's a relief to come up against the blamelessly innocent character played by Elvis Presley ... never has his sulky charm been so much in evidence.

The Sunday Telegraph

 Follow That Dream

A light comedy in which the Kwimpers, a hillbilly-style family always on the move in their ancient car, decide to homestead in Florida despite opposition from local townsfolk. Elvis successfully plays it for laughs as the eldest son Toby.

Studio: United Artists
Released: May 1962
Producer: David Weisbart

Director: Gordon Douglas
Format: De Luxe color/Panavision
Leads: Elvis Presley, Arthur O'Connell, Anne Helm

Above: **Front-of-house still, Follow That Dream, May 1962**

One of the front-of-house stills that used to be displayed outside cinemas, showing a selection of shots from the film playing at the time.

THE MIRISCH COMPANY presents

ELViS Presley as KiD Galaha

COLOR by DE LUXE Released thru UNITED UA

 ## Kid Galahad

A boxing melodrama—with songs. Elvis is the new kid whose potential in the ring draws the attention of some of the seedier elements of the fight fraternity, who try to pressure him to "throw" the biggest fight of his career.

Studio: United Artists
Released: August 1962
Producer: David Weisbart

Director: Phil Karlson
Format: De Luxe color
Leads: Elvis Presley, Gig Youg, Lola Albright, Charles Bronson

Above: **On set, Kid Galahad, November–December 1961**

For the fight scenes in *Kid Galahad*, Elvis listens to some advice from his boxing coach Mushy Callahan, who was a former junior welterweight champion of the world.

Left: **Still from Girls! Girls! Girls!, 1962**

One of Elvis' many outdoor frolics on film, *Girls! Girls! Girls!* was typical of the bland movies that were to soon become the norm for him. Here he poses with one of his female co-stars, Stella Stevens.

 Girls! Girls! Girls!

A seagoing charter fisherman, Ross Carpenter (Elvis) tries singing in a nightclub to raise money for a boat. He soon gets embroiled romantically with a rich heiress, despite his girlfriend being a singer at the club.

Studio: Paramount
Released: November 1962
Producer: Hal B. Wallis

Director: Norman Taurog
Format: Technicolor
Leads: Elvis Presley, Stella Stevens, Laurel Goodwin

Above: **The World's Fair, Seattle, September 5, 1962**

Filming at the actual World's Fair held in Seattle required that Elvis being escorted by 100 special policemen hired by the studio, MGM. The shoot took place in the midst of the thousands of ordinary members of the public visiting the Fair.

It Happened At The World's Fair

Crop-dusting bush pilot Mike Edwards, played by Elvis, and his sidekick Danny (Gary Lockwood), get involved at the Seattle World's Fair with a temporarily abandoned child and helpful—and predictably attractive—nurse.

Studio: Metro Goldwyn Mayer

Released: April 1963

Producer: Ted Richmond

Director: Norman Taurog

Format: Metrocolor/Panavision

Leads: Elvis Presley, Joan O'Brien, Gary Lockwood

ELVIS PRESLEY

PUÑOS Y LAGRIMAS

PANAVISION · METROCOLOR

JOAN O'BRIEN
GARY LOCKWOOD
VICKY TIU
YVONNE CRAIG

CIRE films

ARGUMENTO:
SI ROSE Y SEAMAN JACOBS · PRODUCTOR:
TED RICHMOND
DIRECTOR: NORMAN TAUROG

Compared with The Beatles, Elvis Presley sounds like Caruso in "Fun in Acapulco"... And he certainly looks better. In fact, this attractive travel poster for the famed Mexican resort is far and away his best musical feature to date... And Mr Presley has never seemed so relaxed and personable.

New York Times

 Fun In Acapulco

Elvis plays an ex-trapeze artist who has lost his nerve, finding a job as a singer-cum-lifeguard at a resort hotel, where the manager—played by Ursula Andress—takes more than a professional interest in him, despite some competition.

Studio: Paramount
Released: November 1963
Producer: Hal B. Wallis

Director: Richard Thorpe
Format: Technicolor
Leads: Elvis Presley, Ursula Andress, Elsa Cardenas

Kissin' Cousins

An Air Force officer confronts a mountain clan while trying to negotiate the takeover of the family's mountain home as a missile base, only to find that he is almost identical to one of the hillbillies, who, it transpires, is a distant cousin.

Studio: **Metro Goldwyn Mayer**
Released: **March 1963**
Producer: **Sam Katzman**

Director: **Gene Nelson**
Format: **Metrocolor, Panavision**
Leads: **Elvis Presley, Arthur O'Connell, Gelda Farrell**

Left: **Publicity shot, Kissin' Cousins, March 1963**

Left to right, a double-take with Yvonne Craig, Elvis, Elvis and Cynthia Pepper. Lance LeGault, who was Elvis' stand-in for many of his movies, recalled how quickly the movies were being turned around: "We shot the picture (Kissin' Cousins) in a little over two weeks; it was a quickie… When they realized they could take this guy and do a film that quickly with him, from then on we were on to quick pictures."

★ Viva Las Vegas

What would otherwise have been a lacklustre film with a mundane plot, this story of a racing driver's adventures in the gambling mecca is enlivened by Elvis' interaction in song, dance, and romance with vivacious Ann-Margret.

Studio: Metro Goldwyn Mayer
Released: April 1964
Producers: Jack Cummings, George Sidney
Director: George Sidney
Format: Metrocolor/Panavision
Leads: Elvis Presley, Ann-Margret

Left: **Still with Ann-Margret, summer, 1963**

Swedish actress Ann-Margret was twenty-two years old, a singer and dancer, blessed with the good looks and sensuality that the camera loved, and seemed made to order for Elvis Presley. Indeed, sparks flew from the first meeting.

Music ignited a fiery pent-up passion inside Elvis and me. It was an odd, embarrassing, funny, inspiring, and wonderful sensation. We looked at each other move and saw virtual mirror images.

Ann-Margret

Right: **Publicity still with Ann-Margret, summer, 1963**

Rumors abounded around the film capital about the two stars having an affair, confirmed later by the memoirs of several of Elvis' entourage. Indeed, the actress apparently leaked to the British press that they were getting engaged (despite Elvis being married at the time) although she hotly denied it later.

Roustabout

An itinerant singer—Elvis, of course—gets a job as a fairground hand and helps rescue the traveling carnival from economic collapse by attracting the crowds with his vocalizing, seeking the help of a fortune teller on the way!

Studio: Paramount
Released: November 1964
Producer: Hal B. Wallls

Director: John Rich
Format: Technicolor/Techniscope
Leads: Elvis Presley, Barbara Stanwyck, Joan Freeman

Left: **Publicity still, Roustabout, 1964**

Despite some mundane reviews, like all Elvis movies Roustabout was a money maker. It grossed three million dollars on its first release, and in 1964 Elvis was ranked as Hollywood's sixth biggest money-making star.

Right: **Still, Elvis and Barbara Stanwyk, Roustabout, March–April 1964**

On the last day of shooting, a story appeared in the *Las Vegas Desert News and Telegram*:

"Would you believe that Richard Burton and Peter O'Toole owe part of their current success [in Becket] to Elvis Presley? Were it not for the revenue from Elvis' movies, there might not have been the wherewithal to film Becket. Says producer Wallis, 'In order to do the artistic pictures, it is necessary to make the commercially successful Presley pictures. But that doesn't mean a Presley picture can't have quality, too.' "

Getting God

Hairdresser, Larry Geller, arrived on the scene as Elvis was wrapping *Roustabout*. After a trim and a tint, Geller and Elvis began to talk; it turned into a four-hour marathon about religion. Geller quit his day job and brought Elvis the first of many theology books. With the same mixture of generosity and tyranny that characterized every new avocation, Elvis involved everyone in his spiritual quest. Suddenly Vegas, Memphis, football games, and girls were all on hold. Inevitably, Elvis' entourage regarded Geller with resentment and suspicion. Geller was dubbed "Rasputin" and "the Swami." In Memphis, Priscilla and Vernon had a similar reaction to Geller's influence.

Elvis pursued his studies undeterred. He read in Memphis, on breaks between shots on films, into the night. Each new solution brought more questions. For a man who had conquered the world at twenty-one, this quest for meaning was overwhelming. Finally, driving through the New Mexican desert, with Geller at his side, Elvis had a revelation while gazing at the clouds:

> "Elvis swung the bus over to the roadside and brought it to a violent halt. 'Just follow me, Larry!' he shouted as he bolted out the door and began running across the sand. I finally caught up, and as we stood in the cool desert breeze Elvis' face beamed with joy.
>
> " 'It's God!' he cried. 'It's God!' Tears streamed down his face as he hugged me tightly and said, '…I thank you from the bottom of my heart. You got me here. I'll never forget, never, man. It really happened. I saw the face of Stalin and I thought to myself, Why Stalin? Is it a projection of something that's inside of me? Is God trying to show me what he thinks of me?…And then it happened! The face of Stalin turned right

Right: **Elvis and Larry Geller, 1966**

Larry Geller first met Elvis when he stood in for his regular hairdresser Sal Orifice in May 1964.

into the face of Jesus, and he smiled at me, and every fiber of my being felt it. For the first time in my life, God and Christ are a living reality. Oh, God. Oh, God,' Elvis kept saying. Then he paused and added a peculiar aside, 'Can you imagine what the fans would think if they saw me like this?'

'They'd only love you all the more,' I said.

'Yeah,' he said, 'well, I hope that's true.' "

There was a yearning in Elvis, a thirst for meaning that battled desperately with the product he was fast becoming. No one was more suspicious of this newfound spirituality than the Colonel; he regarded Geller as a con man. But Geller, sincere or not, was no match for the drugs, insecurity, and self-styled machismo that would eventually drown Elvis.

Above: **Still from Girl Happy, June–July 1964**

Left to right: Gary Crosby, Elvis Presley, Joby Baker, and Jimmy Hawkins.

 # Girl Happy

An even more implausible plot than any of Elvis' previous movies—if that's possible. Our hero, a singer with a '60s-style "beat group," is hired along with his band to chaperone the beautiful daughter of a Chicago gangster.

Studio: Metro Goldwyn Mayer

Released: April 1965

Producer: Joe Pasternak

Director: Boris Sagal

Format: Metrocolor/Panavision

Leads: Elvis Presley, Shelley Fabares, Gary Crosby

Tickle Me

A rodeo rider waiting for the season to start takes a job at a dude ranch/health spa—cue plenty of pretty girls—where he helps the physical training instructor (who he ends up marrying) escape from a gang of villains after hidden treasure.

Studio: Allied Artists
Released: November 1965
Producer: Ben Schwalb
Director: Norman Taurog
Format: De Luxe color/Panavision
Leads: Elvis Presley, Julie Adams, Jocelyn Lane

VIS take on the rodeo...the robbers...and the Ghost House!

Right: **Graceland, March 1965**

Elvis with one of several Cadillac automobiles on the driveway outside Graceland. These photos and others from the session accompanied a newspaper interview in which Elvis explained his need for privacy: "I certainly haven't lost my respect for my fans, I withdraw not from my fans but from myself."

(Sam Katzman) was on my ass, really giving me a rough time... Elvis came over and said, "Can I talk to you for a minute?" I said, "You bet. Sit down." He said, "It's getting a little rough out there, isn't it?" I said, "Yeah, but nothing for you to worry about. This is my problem. I don't want this to affect you or your performance in any way at all. I'll take care of it." Elvis was such an aware and considerate person. He said, "I just wanted you to know, if they're not giving you enough time to do this picture right, I can get sick in such a hurry you'd be surprised."

Gene Nelson, director

 Harum Scarum

An American actor Johnny Tyrone (Elvis) visits the fictional Middle Eastern country of Lunakahn, where various far-fetched adventures take place before Johnny returns to Las Vegas with a bevy of belly-dancing beauties.

Studio: **Metro Goldwyn Mayer**
Director: **Gene Nelson**
Released: **November 1965**

Format: **Metrocolor**
Producer: **Sam Katzman**
Leads: **Elvis Presley, Mary Ann Mobley, Fran Jeffries**

AVVENTURA in ORIENTE

(HAREM HOLIDAY)

MARY ANN MOBLEY · FRAN JEFFRIES
MICHAEL ANSARA

scritto da
GERALD DRAYSON ADAMS

diretto da
GENE NELSON

prodotto da
SAM KATZMAN

una produzione
FOUR LEAF

in M TR COLOR

255

Paradise Hawaiian Style

This time Elvis plays an airline pilot with girl trouble, who loses his license after a minor accident. He teams up with a partner in an inter-island helicopter business, bringing more thrills, romance, and songs.

Studio: Paramount
Released: July 1966
Producer: Hal B. Wallis

Director: Michael Moore
Format: Technicolor
Leads: Elvis Presley, Suzanna Leigh

Left: **On location, Paradise Hawaiian Style, August 1966**

Elvis on location in Hawaii, getting to know some of his local admirers a little better. Whenever a movie was been shot on outdoor location, Elvis, the Colonel, and the film's director and crew, would conduct a fine balancing act between the needs of privacy and security on the set and the public relations necessity of meeting and greeting the inevitable crowds of fans.

Left: **Frankie and Johnny, 1966**
Another story, another hat. Elvis is seen here in parade-style bandsman's uniform in *Frankie and Johnny*, a cinematic version of the old folk song. Costume-wise it certainly wasn't "Blue Suede Shoes!"

Frankie And Johnny

Frankie and Johnny are a Mississippi river boat singing duo. Frankie won't marry Johnny till he gives up gambling; Johnny is tempted by the fiery Nellie Blye; and Frankie shoots Johnny. But he survives and they are reunited to live happily ever after.

Studio: **United Artists**

Released: **March 1966**

Producer: **Edward Small**

Director: **Frederick de Cordova**

Format: **Technicolor**

Leads: **Elvis Presley, Donna Douglas**

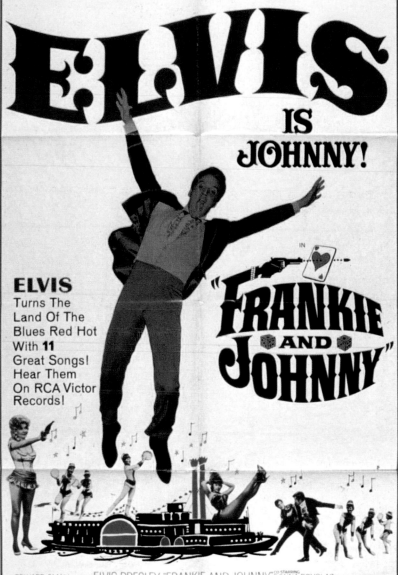

To be honest, I'd describe Elvis on that showing as a boring old fart, but I do know Ringo enjoyed his game of pool.

Tony Barrow, Beatles press officer

Right: **The Beatles, 1965**

When The Beatles met Elvis at his Bel Air home on August 27, 1965, the British group—the biggest pop stars in the world at the time—autographed this photograph for long-time Elvis friend and assistant Jerry Schilling, who was present at the legendary meeting.

Above: **On set, Spinout, February–March 1966**

Elvis climbs out of a racing car during the shooting for Spinout, with the crew and others looking on.

 **Spinout**

Mike McCoy (Elvis) is a rock'n'roll singer whose other great passions are girls and racing formula cars. In this last pursuit he rises to the challenge of driving a car in a race, and gets involved in various romantic adventures on the way.

Studio: Metro Goldwyn Mayer

Released: November 1966

Producer: Joe Pasternak

Director: Norman Taurog

Format: Metrocolor/Panavision

Leads: Elvis Presley, Shelley Fabares, Deborah Walley, Diane McBain

Above: **Still from Spinout, February–March 1966**

Diane McBain plays best-selling writer Diana St. Clair, who has vowed to marry Elvis' character, Mike McCoy, if he wins the race.

How great thou art!

For the May 1966 session in Nashville, Elvis hired eleven vocalists, including The Jordanaires and childhood idol, Jake Hess, from The Statesmen (now heading the quartet, The Imperials). RCA asked Felton Jarvis, who had produced Gladys Knight and Fats Domino, to man the booth. Jarvis, who'd been inspired by early Elvis records to go into music, was ecstatic. When Jarvis and Elvis met, the energy was palpable.

Time stood still as Elvis and the eleven singers filled the room with joy and beauty. Eleven takes of "Run On" built to a crescendo, impossible to eclipse—until they did. "How Great Thou Art" was the next number, Elvis yielding himself completely to the passion. Exhausted, many of the vocalists had to leave. But Elvis soared, oblivious to everything except the spirit that moved him. He cut almost an entire gospel album, belted out a romping version of The Clover's hit "Down in the Alley," and switched gears again, capturing the moody introspection of Bob Dylan's "Tomorrow is a Long Time," even though Elvis detested Dylan's voice (a recurring drollery of Elvis' was that his mouth felt "like Bob Dylan's been sleeping in it"). Everyone was drained, except for the two men who started it all. When the secretaries came to open the studio the next morning, they found Jarvis and Elvis, deep in conversation. Three more nights of magic ensued.

Easy Come, Easy Go

Elvis plays a navy frogman, Ted Jackson, who is searching for sunken treasure in the wreck of an old vessel. His quest leads him to a yoga and meditation class, where he meets the heiress to a fortune.

Studio: Paramount

Released: March 1967

Producer: Joseph Huzen, Hal B. Wallis

Director: John Rich

Format: Technicolor

Leads: Elvis Presley, Dodie Marshall

Above: **Still from Double Trouble, April 1967**

Elvis gets into the flamenco spirit during a carnival in Antwerp, one of the
European ports of call in *Double Trouble*.

 Double Trouble

Society entertainer Guy Lambert, performing in London, is pursued by an attractive
young student and an equally beguiling rich heiress, in travels involving jewel thieves
in the Belgian cities of Bruges, Brussels, and Antwerp.

Studio: Metro Goldwyn Mayer

Released: April, 1967

Producer: Judd Bernard, Irwin Winkler

Director: Norman Taurog

Format: Metrocolor/Panavision

Leads: Elvis Presley, Annette Day,
John Williams, Yvonne Roman

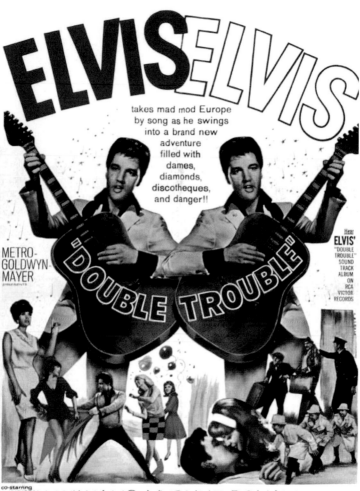

ELVIS ELVIS

takes mad mod Europe
by song as he swings
into a brand new
adventure
filled with
dames,
diamonds,
discotheques,
and danger!!

Hear
ELVIS'
"DOUBLE
TROUBLE"
SOUND
TRACK
ALBUM
ON
RCA
VICTOR
RECORDS

METRO-
GOLDWYN-
MAYER
PRESENTS

"DOUBLE TROUBLE"

co-starring
JOHN WILLIAMS   YVONNE ROMAIN
The WIERE BROS. and introducing ANNETTE DAY

SCREEN PLAY BY   BASED ON A & STORY BY   DIRECTED BY   PRODUCED BY
JO HEIMS   MARC BRANDEL   NORMAN TAUROG · JUDD BERNARD and IRWIN WINKLER
IN **PANAVISION®** and **METROCOLOR**

269

Right: **Aladdin Hotel, Las Vegas, May 1, 1967**
Elvis and Priscilla were married by Nevada
State Supreme Court Justice David Zenoff, who
said of the bride and groom: "He was most
respectful and so nervous he was almost
bawling. Then I was taken over to meet
Priscilla. She was absolutely petrified …
couldn't open her mouth." In the picture
Priscilla is flanked by Elvis and her sister,
Michelle Beaulieu.

Right: **Aladdin Hotel, Las Vegas, May 1, 1967**

Elvis and Priscilla posing with their wedding cake and a group of music executive guests (L–R): Tom Diskin, Colonel Parker's right hand man; Graylun Landun of RCA; unidentified; Harry Jenkins of RCA (at back); Irv Schechtor, William Morris Agency (front); unidentified; Abe Lastfogel, Chairman of William Morris Agency (next to Priscilla); and Freddy Bienstock, of the Hill and Range music publishing company.

Above: **Aladdin Hotel, Las Vegas, May 1, 1967**

Newlyweds Elvis and Priscilla toast each other after the ceremony.

Right: **Las Vegas, May 1, 1967**

Elvis and his bride smile happily as they prepare to board a chartered jet airplane after their marriage, bound for a honeymoon at the recently purchased Flying Circle G ranch in Mississippi.

We were in Nashville cutting the soundtrack for "Clambake" in 1967 with The Jordanaires, and Elvis told them, "Y'all sing on the chorus with me." Well, the director of the picture was there, and he said, "Elvis, I don't think you understand where the song's going to be used in the picture. In this particular scene, you're riding down the highway on a motorcycle singing this song. The voices can't sing along with you. Where would we put the singers?" Elvis thought a second and said, "Put 'em the same damn place you put the band." That was the end of that.

Felton Jarvis, producer

 # Clambake

A "trading places" storyline has Elvis as a bored rich boy, wanting to pursue his own thing in life rather than the family oil business. He swaps identities with a Miami water-ski instructor with predictable and chaotic results.

Studio: United Artlsts

Released: November 1967

Producer: Arnold Lavan, Arthur Gardner, Jules Levy

Director: Arthur H. Nadel

Format: Technicolor/Techniscope

Leads: Elvis Presley, Shelley Fabares

This is the greatest thing that has ever happened to me.

Elvis announcing Priscilla is pregnant, July 1967

Right: **Elvis, Priscilla, and Lisa Marie, February 5, 1968**

Elvis and Priscilla in a photo shoot for the press as they are about to leave the Baptist Memorial Hospital, Memphis with their new daughter, Lisa Marie, born February 1, 1968.

Right: **Flamingo Hotel, Las Vegas, April 6, 1968**

There was instant rapport when Elvis met the Welsh singer Tom Jones. Fresh from his hit song "What's New Pussycat?" Jones was still fairly unknown in the United States and his first meeting with Elvis was totally exhilarating for the young singer: "He sorta waved over in my direction, and I thought, 'Is he waving at me?' Just in case he was, I waved back! It was strange, you know, because I had never seen the man before. Then he came over and said hello and said he knew every track on my album! We chatted for a while and I asked him, 'Any chance I can get a photograph together with you for the British newspapers?' He said, 'Of course.' Then, as we were doing the photographs, he started singing songs off my album! I was really dumbfounded. I was thrilled that he even knew who I was. Our friendship started right then."

Elvis hated most of those later films. I mean, in "Stay Away Joe" they had him singing to a bull!

Red West

 ## Stay Away Joe

Not for the first time in his film career, Elvis plays a Native American. Joe Lightcloud is a hard-living, hard-drinking guy who has ambitions to become a cattle baron, but seems more interested in chasing girls than running a herd.

Studio: Metro Goldwyn Mayer
Released: March 1968
Producer: Douglas Laurence

Director: Peter Tewksbury
Format: Metrocolor/Panavision
Leads: Elvis Presley, Burgess Meredith, Joan Blondell, Katy Jurado, Thomas Gomez

Above: **Still from Speedway, June 1968**

Nancy Sinatra, who was a singing star in her own right, got to duet with Elvis in one number in the film, as well as having a solo spot herself.

This is, after all, just another Presley movie—which makes no use at all of one of the most talented, important, and durable performers of our time. Music, youth, and customs were much changed by Elvis Presley twelve years ago. From the twenty-six movies he has made since he sang "Heartbreak Hotel" you would never guess it.

New York Times, reviewing Speedway

 **Speedway**

In yet another unlikely plot, Elvis is a stock-car racing driver who gets on the wrong side of the tax man, or in this case tax woman, in the shapely form of Nancy Sinatra. Soon, of course, it's him chasing her as love blossoms.

Studio: Metro Goldwyn Mayer
Released: June 1968
Producer: Douglas Laurence

Director: Norman Taurog
Format: Metrocolor/Panavision
Leads: Elvis Presley, Nancy Sinatra, Bill Bixby

From dawn
to darkroom...
from doll to doll...
ELVIS clicks
with the chicks
as a playboy
photographer
who leads a
double-life!

Above: **Still from Live A Little, Love A Little, October 1968**

Elvis' photographer character in *Live A Little, Love A Little*, Greg Nolan, contemplates the over-the-top décor in a *Playboy* bunny-style advertising agency.

Live A Little, Love A Little

The chance of a potentially frothy comedy is wasted in this tale of a Los Angeles newspaper photographer who gets involved with a love-hungry woman with many aliases—and men—and her pet Great Dane, Albert.

Studio: Metro Goldwyn Mayer
Released: October 1968
Producer: Douglas Laurence

Director: Norman Taurog
Format: Metrocolor/Panavision
Leads: Elvis Presley, Michele Carey, Don Porter, Rudy Vallee

'68 comeback

The day that he was released from *Live a Little, Love a Little*, Elvis began discussing the Christmas special with executive producer, Bob Finkel. Finkel recruited Steve Binder and partner Bones Howe (who had worked with Elvis at the Radio Recorders studio back in the mid fifties). Recently Binder and Howe had shot an innovative Petula Clark TV special. Instead of an hour on a bare stage spitting out the latest Christmas single, they suggested Elvis take this opportunity to show everyone who he really was. Elvis, initially polite, got worked up enough to be "scared to death," a good sign. The Colonel, assured of his soundtrack and a Christmas single, shrugged his shoulders and gave the go-ahead.

Binder and Howe, together with musical arranger Billy Goldenberg, worked furiously on a script that would tell Elvis' story. Elvis immediately clicked with costume designer Bill Belew's ideas for a black leather suit and high "Napoleonic" collars. He was less enthused about a gold lame suit that would hearken back to the suit that the Colonel had designed for Elvis in the fifties. They struck a compromise: Elvis would wear the jacket with black tuxedo pants.

One of the highlights of the special occurred by accident. Inspired by the clique that formed in Elvis' room after rehearsals, Binder designed a small stage, along the lines of a stylized boxing ring. Scotty Moore and D.J. Fontana were flown in.

It was the finest music of his life. If ever there was music that bleeds, this was it.

Greil Marcus

Elvis, Scotty, D.J., along with some members of the Memphis Mafia, sat around jamming on "Guitar Man," sharing anecdotes and tunes. Oddly, the almost claustrophobic size of the stage was an inspiration. Elvis, long hemmed in by the relentless toil of insipid movies and worse soundtracks, was here restricted only by space, confined to showing only himself—and was set free.

The genesis for another segment was a tragic one. The news of Bobby Kennedy's assassination hit Elvis hard, as had the murder of Martin Luther King, Jr. The producers, struck with the depth of Elvis' grief, decided to buck the Colonel's demand for a Christmas song conclusion. Instead, the hastily written "If I Can Dream" was presented to Elvis as a way for him to express his anguished hopes for the future. Elvis confirmed their expectations: "We're doing it," he declared. And he did. Elvis transcended the somewhat pallid good intentions of the song with pure guts, his vocals fueled by the passion of his conviction.

The entire show was a masterpiece. And the master knew it. Elvis (who before the show had experienced stage fright so severe that he initially refused to go on) was so high and mighty that he defied the gods—or god. He called the Colonel into his dressing room. As Belew extricated him from the sweat-drenched leather suit, Elvis looked Parker in the eye and flatly stated, "I want to tour again. I want to go out and work with a live audience." Everyone in that room believed Elvis. And for once, he believed himself.

Elvis was thrilled when he viewed the final cut of *Singer Presents Elvis*. (The program was sponsored by Singer sewing machines.) The only one not pleased was the Colonel, who was incensed that not one Christmas song was included. He threatened to pull out unless his Yuletide demands were met, and an impromptu version of "Blue Christmas" quickly replaced Elvis' blistering version of "Tiger Man."

The press reviews were mixed, but fascinated. And the ratings were even more heartening: *Singer Presents Elvis* was the number one show of the season and gave NBC its biggest overall ratings victory that year, also winning a Peabody award. "If I Can Dream" was released as a single and stayed in the charts for over three months, reaching #12. *Singer Presents Elvis* was quickly dubbed for all time "the '68 Comeback."

Left and following page: **Singer Presents Elvis, June 1968**

In both the intimate sets performed before a live audience, and the more ambitious studio set pieces, Elvis shined as he hadn't for a good six years.

Above: **Singer Presents Elvis, June 1968**
Elvis wears a gold lamé jacket as he sings "Trouble." The special aired on
December 3, 1968, and was repeated on August 17, 1969.

Right: **Singer Presents Elvis, June 1968**
The opening sequence of the "comeback" special, in which Elvis "lookalikes,"
Jailhouse Rock-style, frame his opening number "Guitar Man."

I was sort of embarrassed for Elvis in some of the movies because of the poor quality of the stories and everything. But, God, at the same time, the guy was so electrifying. I mean, you couldn't watch him on the screen without being riveted.

Don Robertson, songwriter

 **Charro!**

Despite being a non-musical movie (there was just one song, over the credits) this tale of a desperado-turned-Deputy Sheriff—Elvis with a beard—isn't the "ground breaker" it might have been, and met with bad reviews all around.

Studio: National General
Released: March 1968
Producer: Harry Caplan,
Charles Marquis Warren

Director: Charles Marquis Warren
Format: Technicolor
Leads: Elvis Presley, Ina Balin

Elvis and Marilyn Mason start off in constant battle over Chautauqua's "union ri[...]

MGM Presents **"THE TROUBLE WITH**

ip in a romance.

S" PANAVISION®
and METROCOLOR

69/18

 The Trouble With Girls

The manager of a traveling medicine show in the 1920s (The Chautaqua Company, the original title of the film), Elvis gets involved in a small-town murder mystery, as well as with the attractive singer/dancer who wants to unionize the tent show.

Studio: Metro Goldwyn Mayer
Released: September 1969
Producer: Lester Welch
Director: Peter Tewksbury
Format: Metrocolor/Panavision
Leads: Elvis Presley, Marlyn Mason, Sheree North

He confessed right from the start that he'd had a crush on me since the Dick Van Dyke Show. He was so shy about it, he was literally kicking at the dirt below him as he talked. I was his last leading lady. The King would slyly say later on, "I slept with every one of my leading ladies but one." I don't want to bust anyone's cover, but I know who the "one" is.

Mary Tyler Moore

 Change Of Habit

In his final fictional movie, Elvis plays a doctor working in a tough inner-city neighborhood clinic. He accepts the help of three young women, not realizing they are novice nuns in secular attire, and gets romantically involved with one of them.

Studio: Universal
Released: November 1969
Producer: Joe Connelly
Director: William Graham

Format: Technicolor
Leads: Elvis Presley, Mary Tyler Moore, Barbara McNair

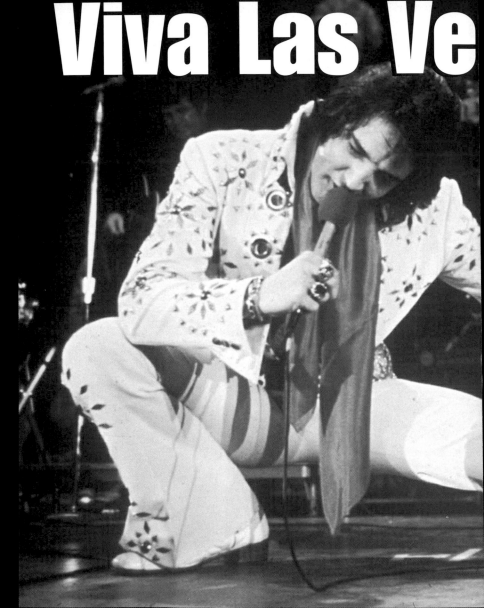

Viva Las Ve

In person 1969–1977

He strode onstage at Vegas' International Hotel, July 31, 1969 facing an invitation-only, celebrity-studded audience. Fats Domino, Cary Grant, Petula Clark, and Burt Bacharach were there, alongside personal supporters—Priscilla, Vernon, producer Felton Jarvis, and a planeload of critics. Perhaps the most meaningful guest was his old mentor, Sam Phillips, to whom Elvis had extended a special invitation. By the time The Sweet Inspirations began their intro, Elvis wasn't sure he could go on. He was that nervous. It wasn't as if he hadn't done his homework. He was prepared, but frightened. For the first time in a while, he cared. Backstage afterward, Elvis was ebullient, and the Colonel had tears in his eyes. Elvis still had it, more than enough of it.

As the shows progressed, Elvis digressed. The onstage patter became looser. The Colonel worried that Elvis was sometimes a little too blue for family shows, but Elvis ignored the warnings. This wasn't *Elvis for Everyone*. This Elvis was for him. And this Elvis was the most successful act in Vegas history. The reviews raved; the International Hotel gave him a $25,000 per week raise for the next engagement.

But the months preceding his January 1970 Vegas encore revealed troubles in the wings. Elvis was increasingly estranged from Priscilla, who busied herself with self-improvement classes and Lisa Marie. Karate had been a part of his life since the army, but now he reunited with karate instructor, Ed Parker and the kenpo tradition, practicing ferociously, if intermittently. He reunited also with Daya Mata from the Self Realization Fellowship, confessing his need for love, his desire to lead young people on the right path. And there were the pills. Always the pills when nothing else could fill the days.

So January of 1970 was a release. He enthusiastically threw himself into rehearsals, hiring piano player Glen D. Hardin and drummer Bob Lanning. The song list evolved; the Colonel was looking for a live LP from this gig, revisiting the formula of a film and soundtrack. Confined by a movie script for ten years, he'd been encouraged to ad lib for the TV special. In Vegas, more of his personality was creeping into the shows. Orchestral and heartstrings were plucked with numbers such as "In the Ghetto," "Don't Cry Daddy," "Walk a Mile in My Shoes," and the brand-new single "Kentucky Rain." His costumes evolved into the jumpsuits. He incorporated more karate moves in his dancing. His vulnerability was more practiced; he forgot the words to songs more—it was charming. It was like his life was moving more and more onto the stage.

Felton Jarvis, the man behind Elvis at RCA and who orchestrated the sessions at American, now took a leap of faith in Elvis that many considered foolhardy. He quit his job as a staff producer at RCA to produce Elvis exclusively. For every master he delivered for RCA he would receive $750 and a two percent royalty override. The catch was that he pledged to deliver no less than fifteen sides from Elvis' upcoming recording session, and Elvis' unpredictability, combined with the often disappointing material he was confined to, made that pledge a real challenge.

Jarvis rose to the occasion with the help of men who'd founded The Muscle Shoals soul sound—drummer Jerry Carrigan, bass player Norman Putnam, and keyboardist David Briggs. Perhaps spurred on by the risk his friend Jarvis was taking, Elvis cut thirty-four masters in five nights, giving RCA more than enough material for his new LP, and getting a solid collection for the beginnings of a concept album—*Elvis Country*.

The reviews from the Vegas engagements continued to be enthusiastic, his August 1970 show surmounting the distraction of five Panavision cameras. MGM was filming *Elvis: That's the Way It Is*. Despite the Colonel's perennial disappointment at "not enough Elvis," this film captures the enormous apparatus required to produce an Elvis show, and it illustrates how beautifully Elvis fulfilled all the expectations Vegas had of him.

Another, more serious distraction was the paternity suit leveled at Elvis on August 14 of that year. Although the case was dismissed, it was clear to everyone around Elvis that his marriage vows, never adhered to, were by now almost nonexistent.

Priscilla was well aware of the state of her marriage. She had always been locked away like the good china, brought out for appearances. But she was beginning to change; the decorating and calligraphy classes were no longer filling the void. She had begun taking karate classes to help bring her closer to Elvis and she wound up meeting the man she would soon fall in love with—handsome karate instructor, Mike Stone.

Friedrich Nietzsche came to the Sahara Tahoe, July 20, 1971, and he wore a jumpsuit. It was here that music director Joe Guercio introduced Elvis's most famous entrance. An offhand comment from his wife led him to the same idea that Elvis had been toying with. The musical theme for Stanley Kubrick's 1968 film *2001: A Space Odyssey* was an adaptation of Richard Strauss's nineteenth century musical ode to Nietzche's work, *Also sprach Zarathustra*. Its five bold opening notes embody the ascension of man into spheres reserved for the gods. What better way, reasoned Guercio, to introduce Elvis to the stage?

Priscilla finally left Elvis after Christmas of 1972, taking Lisa Marie. Elvis had his Washington D.C. girlfriend flown in for his birthday; he was thirty-seven. But at his January Vegas engagement, he was more subdued. Ballads such as Marty Robbins' "You Gave Me a Mountain," about a wife and child leaving a marriage, were sung with particular fervor.

After touring for a couple weeks in 1970 and 1971, Elvis decided to hit the road in earnest. To whet appetites, the Colonel had MGM film the spring 1972 tour. They hired Bob Abel and Pierre Adidge, who'd triumphed with their documentary of the 1970 Joe Cocker tour, *Mad Dogs and Englishmen*. After filming the gig in Buffalo, they showed the raw footage to the Colonel, who was jubilant: "Go out there and make the best Elvis film ever." They followed the tour through four cities, capturing the excitement of the opening date, and the increasing refinement and lack of energy in subsequent shows. Lighting for *Elvis on Tour* was arranged to downplay Elvis' bloated appearance.

On July 26, 1972, Priscilla and Elvis were legally separated. Reports about Mike Stone broke soon after, just as Elvis was beginning his August Vegas engagement. During his frequent dalliances outside his marriage, the news about Mike Stone was a shock, and a very public humiliation. His drug use was stepped up; there were doctors running in and out of his suite at the Hilton, and his speech was often alarmingly slurred.

Despite the impending divorce, Elvis had a constant string of belles in tow; he settled on a Memphis beauty queen—twenty-two year old Linda Thompson. Linda was not only pretty, she was both innocent enough not to be wary of Elvis' drug use, and loyal enough to stick around after she understood its extent. Everyone around Elvis was happy with Linda. And, for a long time, she was happy with Elvis, with reservations.

The difficulties in his personal life were still eclipsed by the success he was enjoying. The Madison Square Garden album went gold, while "Burning Love" became his first million seller in two years. The good news fueled an ambition long harbored by the Colonel: a television concert broadcast globally via satellite. Honolulu was the chosen site; the time zone made it convenient to reach Asia, Africa, and Australia. *Aloha from Hawaii* became the first entertainment special to be beamed worldwide.

His weight ballooned after the Honolulu spectacular, and it was a decidedly different Elvis that was on the Vegas stage, heavier in body and in spirit. Though Linda Thompson was with him, she was unable to prevent the constant doctor visits. Often the only spark in his performances was provided by his resplendent costumes, reflecting the dazzled and adoring gaze of his fans. But his deterioration was evident even with the most devoted fans, and reviews began to feature words like "listless" and "flabby." In February at the Las Vegas Hilton he cancelled the last two midnight shows and walked out during the dinner show, and in April at Lake Tahoe the last four shows were cancelled.

Priscilla was stunned at Elvis' appearance when they showed up at divorce court on October 9. She had renegotiated her settlement from $100,000 to 2 million dollars, plus child support. Vernon was furious, but Elvis was amenable, even passive. Within six days he was in Baptist Memorial Hospital in Memphis. The medications had finally caught up with him.

Linda stayed by his side; the nurses moved in a hospital bed for her. It took two weeks in the hospital and two-and-half months at Graceland to recuperate—the longest period Elvis had gone without working in two years.

Memphis saw its own "in concert" on March 16, 1974. It was the first time he had played there since 1961, and like every other show of that three-week tour, it was sold out. A fifth show was added, producing another live LP. *Elvis Recorded Live on Stage in Memphis* did surprisingly well, selling almost a half a million, and Elvis' live version of "How Great Thou Art" netted him his third Grammy for "Best Inspirational Performance." However, little else was inspiring about the performance. Although touring was great financially, Elvis was obviously tired, bored, and slipping back into the habits that had almost killed him in October.

The opening of his August Vegas engagement was briefly invigorated by a change of venue. The Richard Strauss intro was replaced by a medley of blues numbers, and new material. Despite the positive reviews, the intro reverted back to the original format the next night, as if the show were running Elvis, not the other way around. Elvis seemed progressively run down, and his monologues increasingly ran on, often provoking nervous or embarrassed laughter from the audience. Priscilla, attending closing night with Lisa Marie, was saddened and surprised when he discussed the vagaries of their marriage and divorce onstage, which ended when he screamed out threats to anyone who suggested that he was "strung out": "…if I find or hear an individual that has said that about me, I'm going to break their goddamn neck, you sonofabitch. That is *dangerous*. I will pull your tongue out by the roots. Thank you very much anyway."

By January 29, 1975, he was back in the hospital. The press reported "non-alcohol-related liver problems," as Dr. Nick struggled to get the drug use under control. Linda Thompson, despite the recent and public additions of new girlfriends, was again at his side. On February 5, Vernon had a heart attack.

While in the hospital, Elvis lost ten pounds and appeared in better spirits. Dr. Nick and a nurse were in daily attendance, strictly dispensing the medications. A benefit for victims of a recent tornado in Mississippi was scheduled for May, and Elvis went back to Vegas by March 18. While backstage, Barbra Streisand and Jon Peters made a pitch for him to co-star in their new picture, a remake of *A Star is Born*. Elvis was thrilled, but the Colonel, citing their inexperience and the fact that they would be making a *Barbra Streisand* picture, not an *Elvis Presley* picture, nixed the project. Elvis, initially disappointed, soon lost interest.

Temper tantrums and lacerating jokes were becoming more common. His bass player Duke Bardwell, sick of the constant onstage harassment, simply turned in his TCB pendant and quit. In Norfolk, Virginia, his vulgar comments about soprano (and former lover) Kathy Westmoreland expanded to include his back-up singers. Early in the show, he told the audience that he "smelled green peppers and onions and that … The Sweet Inspirations had probably been eating catfish." There were apologies and extravagant gifts (he spent over $85,000 in jewelry in that week alone).

His gift-giving and spending escalated from there. Jeweler Lowell Hays was now a part of the entourage, catering to Elvis' every whim. One night on tour, Elvis gave an audience member a $6,500 dollar ring, hoping to inspire the reactions that his songs couldn't. Twice he threw his guitar into the audience, stating that he didn't want or need it. Again and again, he had given himself to his audience emotionally and artistically. He seemed to be telling them that material things were all he had left.

The next two years were a blur of embarrassing shows, cancellations, failed recording sessions and broken relationships. Those who stayed felt the taint that comes when watching someone self-destruct. Musical arranger Joe Guercio, once so thrilled with Elvis, turned to friends after a June 1976 Philadelphia concert and said, "You know, all he can do now is die." Sonny and Red West, along with karate expert Dave Hebler, were summarily fired by Vernon in July of 1976. They were given a week's severance pay, without a word from Elvis.

By May of 1977, their book *Elvis: What Happened?* appeared in Australian and British newspapers. It was a harrowing account of Elvis' excesses. Elvis, humiliated and betrayed, retreated further into drugs and isolation. The few dates that Elvis played that summer underscored his decline. A CBS special documented what friends and fans couldn't face. Back-up singer Myrna Smith, who had told boyfriend Jerry Schilling that Elvis looked "really good," burst into tears when she later viewed the finished film. "We were all wearing blinders."

On the afternoon of Tuesday, August 16, girlfriend Ginger Alden noticed that Elvis wasn't in bed. She found him in the bathroom face down, and telephoned for help. The room quickly filled with people trying to resuscitate Elvis, while Vernon keened over his son's body. Dr. Nick arrived in time to work frantically on Elvis as firemen transported them to Baptist Memorial Hospital. But by 3:30 p.m. his death was a certainty, and late that afternoon the announcement was made: Elvis Presley was dead.

The autopsy report was announced that evening by medical examiner Dr. Jerry Franciso. Death was due to "cardiac arrhythmia" he announced, and medical investigator Dan Warlick found a newly emptied and scoured bathroom. But the pathology reports confirmed what everyone already knew. Fourteen drugs were found in Elvis' system, ten in significant quantity.

Elvis was buried at Forest Hill Cemetery, a few hundred yards from Gladys. In the next month, over a million people would visit the gravesite. In October, his body and his mother's were transferred to Graceland, and re-interred in the Meditation Garden. When his father and grandmother died within the next three years, they too were buried there.

Next to Elvis' gravestone, there is a marker smaller than the others, a plaque in memory of Jesse Garon, Elvis' stillborn twin. The man who was told by his mother that he had the strength of two lived only 42 years, but it was a life lived furiously, with passion and grace, glory and shame. There was another woman who had witnessed the birth of Elvis Presley. Marion Keisker, Sam Phillips' assistant, was the first one to record that voice back in 1953. She had watched that Elvis grow into a superstar but was always aware of the fundamental Elvis: "He was like a mirror. Whatever you were looking for, you were going to find in him."

Las Vegas comeback

With guitarist James Burton, who'd led the house band on the popular TV show *Shindig*, Elvis rounded up a fine crew for his "comeback" dates in Las Vegas at the International Hotel, including drummer Ronnie Tutt, rhythm guitarist John Wilkerson, and virtuoso bass player Jerry Scheff, who was turned on by Elvis' commitment during the auditioning process. The black gospel harmonies of The Sweet Inspirations and the white quartet sound of The Imperials were added to the mix. Bill Belew was back, creating the same look that had served Elvis so well on the TV special. Rehearsals were extemporaneous, but very fruitful. Elvis worked feverishly, always maintaining the courteous, patient manner that endeared him to his fellow musicians. The television special, the sessions at American Studio, even the long soul-numbing years in Hollywood had built up to this moment, when he strode onto the stage virtually unannounced, and began "Blue Suede Shoes." It was like no other performer, like no other performance. It was spontaneous; it was inevitable. He ripped into Ray Charles' "I Got a Woman," then onto "All Shook Up," all the numbers delivered with an energy and a control that maddened the audience. "Don't Be Cruel," "Suspicious Minds," "Tiger Man." The waitresses were swooning. He hadn't just come back; he was resurrected.

Right: **International Hotel, Las Vegas, August 1969**

The success of his return to the Las Vegas stage was better than anybody expected. At a press conference the morning after his July 31 opening, Elvis confessed he was, "A little nervous for the first three songs, but then I thought 'What the heck, get with it man, or you might be out of a job tomorrow.' "

When I got out I did a few more movies, and a few more movies, and I got into a rut. You know, there's this big rut just the other side of Hollywood Boulevard...

Left: **Elvis and Lisa Marie, 1970**

This family photograph was taken in December 1970, not long before Lisa Marie's third birthday.

Above and left: **Karate and guns, early 1970s**

By the early 1970s Elvis was devoting much of his leisure time to the martial arts, both in the form of karate—he achieved "master of the art" status—and by collecting and practicing with an ever-burgeoning collection of firearms.

Houston Astrodome

Buoyed by the smash hit of the first Vegas appearance, the Colonel booked Elvis for his first live non-Vegas performance since 1961. The Colonel never did things small; the venue was the Houston Astrodome's Livestock Show and Rodeo. The first of the six shows was a disappointment; the sound quality was terrible and the paltry audience of 16,000 left Elvis crestfallen. "I guess I just can't bring it in like I used to," he conceded. But 36,299 fans proved him wrong in the evening show, and he blasted through the poor acoustics, delivering a performance that was "masterful," according to the *Los Angeles Times*. The next night the crowd was even bigger, managing to break the record for an indoor rodeo performance in any arena. Elvis was making history again.

A live concert to me is exciting because of all the electricity that is generated in the crowd and on stage. It's my favorite part of the business—live concerts.

Right: **Press conference, Houston Astrodome, March 1, 1970**

At a press conference following his final show in Houston, Elvis was presented with a limited edition Rolex watch, a gold deputy sheriff's badge and a Stetson hat, Texas style.

The Memphis mafia

In the fall of 1970, Priscilla and Elvis designed a logo: the letters "TCB" framing a lightening bolt. Long a slang expression in the black community, TCB stood for "taking care of business." The lightning bolt had fascinated Elvis since his childhood. It was, after all, a lightning bolt that transformed unassuming Billy Bratson into superhero Captain Marvel. What else would a superstar have on his logo? Elvis had the logo made into gold necklaces for his closest male friends; initially they were a coveted symbol of Elvis' trust and friendship. The following year he had the ladies' version made with the letters "TLC" (tender loving care). Memphis jeweler Lowell Hays eventually took on the job of making the necklaces, which soon adorned the chests of many Elvis friends and acquaintances. In a flash, it seemed as if the symbol of his attachment became a mass-marketed item.

Above: **The "Memphis mafia," Graceland, December 28, 1970**

After the wedding of old buddy Sonny West, all the entourage repaired to Graceland, where Elvis had this photo taken with "the guys." They are seen here displaying their recently acquired deputy badges, courtesy of the local Shelby County sheriff. Standing, left to right, are Billy Smith, ex-sheriff Bill Morris, Lamar Fike, Jerry Schilling, Sheriff Roy Nixon, Vernon Presley, Charlie Hodge, Sonny West, George Klein, Marty Lacker; and front, left to right, Dr George "Nick" Nichopoulus, Elvis and Red West.

You talk to a lot of people who'll say discipline makes a star. Horseshit! Charisma makes a star. Sinatra, Michael Jackson, Streisand—he walked out there, and there was a whole other feel. He could walk across the stage and not even have to open his mouth.

Joe Guercio, musical arranger

Previous page: **International Hotel Conference Center, August 4, 1970**

Elvis prepares for another season at the International Hotel, Las Vegas. The rehearsals, which took place in the hotel's Conference Center and the main show room, were filmed as part of the movie documentary *Elvis: That's The Way It Is*. The backing orchestra was led by the International's new musical director, Joe Guercio, who despite initial reservations, was highly impressed by Elvis' natural charisma and professionalism.

Right: **International Hotel, Las Vegas, August 1970**

Despite *Cashbox* magazine remarking that "Elvis' show lacked the excitement of previous years," the shows were marked by a new-found spontaneity in Elvis' stage act.

You have no idea how great he is, really you don't. You have no comprehension—it's absolutely impossible. I can't tell you why he's so great, but he is. He's sensational.

Phil Spector

Left: **International Hotel, Las Vegas, August 1970**
Elvis received the good and the great into his dressing room throughout the Vegas season. Here he meets with his old Hollywood friend from the days of *Love Me Tender*, singer Sammy Davis Jr.

Left and below: **On tour, 1970**

Between the 1970 summer and 1971 winter Vegas dates, Elvis toured extensively, developing his act in the increasingly flamboyant jumpsuits that became the Elvis Presley trademark forever after.

The President and the King

Long coveting a badge from the Bureau of Narcotics and Dangerous Drugs (now called the D.E.A.), Elvis sought a meeting with its director, John Ingersoll. When that was unsuccessful, Elvis went over his head to the Executive Chief. On the plane he worked on a letter of introduction to President Nixon, indicating his patriotism and his desire to be of help in reaching young people: "I can and will do more good if I were made a Federal Agent at Large, and I will help but by doing it my way through my communications with people of all ages. First and foremost I am an entertainer but all I need is the Federal credentials."

The White House called Presley and arranged a meeting with the President. Elvis, leaving Sonny and Jerry in the outer office, walked in and introduced himself, presenting Nixon with his credentials—his various law enforcement badges, his cufflinks and the gold belt that he had received from the International Hotel in Vegas. After a short speech pledging his allegiance to the drug war and some mild Beatles bashing, he came to his point. Could he have a BNDD badge to aid him in creating the drug-free world for which both he and Nixon strived? Nixon agreed. Elvis Presley then set another precedent when he embraced history's least huggable Commander-in-Chief. The president awkwardly patted Elvis' shoulder. His confidence back, Elvis introduced Sonny and Jerry. The President gave the boys cufflinks and tie clasps adorned with the Presidential seal. Elvis also urged the President to provide some Oval Office trinkets for the wives. By the next night he was back at Graceland, his new badge confirming what he had always known: he was the King, his wish was everyone's command.

Left: **Elvis and Nixon, The White House, December 21, 1970**

For his meeting with President Nixon, Elvis wore a high-collared white shirt, purple velvet V-neck with matching pants, two gold pendants, his Vegas International gold belt, oversized jeweled aviator glasses, and an Edwardian jacket draped across his shoulders. The president wore a dark suit and a fixed smile.

All he needs is a glance over the shoulder and a whole quadrant of the audience is screaming, jumping up, begging for that tiger's smile to be aimed a little more closely at them.

Greg Shaw, reviewing the Detroit, Michigan show, December 1972

Left: **Elvis on stage, 1975**

Elvis in an outfit that reflected a Native North American influence in the design, seen here with top session guitarist James Burton (center) who was later to play with artists as varied as Emmylou Harris and Elvis Costello.

Following page: **Elvis On Tour, spring, 1972**

The capes became a feature of Elvis' outfits from the early 1970s, seen here in a still from the film documentary released in November 1972, *Elvis On Tour*. Elvis had to dispense with the capes eventually, as fans were increasingly grabbing at them, nearly pulling him off stage on occasion.

Right: **Elvis On Tour, 1972**

His shows were becoming an odd mixture of grandiosity and capriciousness. He was increasingly overweight. The jumpsuits were more splendid, the jewelry heavier, the periodic monologues longer. Frequently, poses were struck, as in the intro to "You've Lost That Loving Feeling." Elvis would stand, back to the audience, lit by a single spotlight, turning only when the chorus would kick in. The rigor mortis of superstardom was beginning to take hold; increasingly Elvis was turning into the very first Elvis impersonator.

He would strike those unforgettable Elvis poses. Right leg forward, left leg thrown back shaking to the music and— the flashbulbs went off and the shrieks got higher and the scene more intense—one was struck with the thought that possibly here was the guy who, if he was so inclined, could have made the place fall down... He stood there at the end, his arms stretched out, the great gold cloak giving him wings, a champion, the only one in his class.

Variety

Left: **Madison Square Garden, New York, June 9, 1972**

Elvis Presley had never performed live in New York City, and it was hard to forget the sneers with which New York reviewers had greeted his early career. Nevertheless, when tickets went on sale on May 9, 2000 people mobbed the box office before dawn. Elvis' three shows sold out so quickly that another one was added, making him the first entertainer to sell out four consecutive shows in Madison Square Garden, reaching more than 80,000 people. RCA recorded the concert, and *Elvis as Recorded Live at Madison Square Garden* was in the stores eight days later.

Aloha from Hawaii

Words like "global" and "billion" had to be daunting even to Elvis, who seemed befuddled during the press conference announcing the event. But he quickly got into the spirit when he confabbed with costume designer Belew, offering one of the few suggestions he had ever made: "He came up with the American eagle [as a motif for the jumpsuit he would wear]… We made an American eagle belt for it, a white leather belt about three or four inches wide with four or five ovals with American eagles on them. And, of course, the cape."

Producer-director Marty Pasetta was also intrinsic in setting Elvis on an epic scale; he worked feverishly to redesign the stage and the lighting so that the excitement of the concert could be translated to 1.5 billion living rooms. The Colonel suggested the staged helicopter arrival, and even paid for entertainment for people waiting to get in. That was not the only philanthropic act involved. The concert admission fee was voluntary, the contributions supporting the Kui Lee Cancer Fund (after the Hawaiian songwriter who'd written, "I'll Remember You," recorded by Elvis). The Colonel and Elvis donated $1000 as the kick-off.

Elvis, twenty-five pounds lighter from a crash diet he had undertaken between November and January, was a leaner, if not meaner version of his Vegas self. Still vaguely puffy and pale beneath his Hawaiian tan, he nonetheless delivered a great rehearsal show, pounding out song after song. The fans were delirious, especially when he sailed his cape into the audience. His costume designer Bill Belew was understandably less enthusiastic:

"But when that rehearsal was over I got a phone call from Joe Esposito. It was just one night before the live broadcast. Joe said, 'Bill, you're not going to believe this. Elvis just threw his belt and cape out into the audience!' I said, 'Joe, what are you talking about? He hasn't even done the show yet!' … When I came out of my state of shock, I got on the phone and called everybody involved. That night we cut, embroidered, and did everything—nearly killed ourselves—and I called Joe and said, 'Joe, in half an hour everything will be ready… He said, 'Okay, our plane will be in the air in half an hour to pick him up.' Nicki took everything with him to Hawaii, and they were just wonderful to him. He even went to the show. But later that night, after they'd done the live satellite broadcast, Nicki called me and said, 'Bill, you're not going to believe this!' I said, 'Oh, please, what are you going to tell me now?' He said, 'Elvis threw the belt and the cape into the audience again! I'm getting on the plane, coming back. We've got to make another cape and belt so he can go on with the tour.'

At the time, the belt and cape were each worth about five thousand dollars, so Elvis threw ten thousand dollars into the audience two nights in a row!"

The actual show was a triumph of marketing. Elvis threw out his cape again, casting his spell over the whole world. The projected charity fundraising goal of $25,000 was tripled. The broadcast got the highest rating ever registered in Japan at 37.8 percent of the viewers. Using three pressing plants working overtime, the two-album set was released in a week and a half. In less than a month it had shot to the top of the LP charts, selling half-a-million copies. Colonel Tom wrote to Elvis, "Without your dedication to your following it couldn't have been done."

Above: **Honolulu airport, Hawaii, January 9, 1973**

At the airport in Honolulu, Elvis is presented with the traditional *lei* before being helicoptered to the Hilton Hawaiian Village Hotel.

Left: **Press conference, Las Vegas Hilton, September 4, 1972**

The "Aloha from Hawaii" broadcasts were first announced by Elvis and RCA president Rocco Laginestra at a press conference the previous September, when Elvis was appearing at the Las Vegas Hilton.

It was a thrilling, compact hour—long on music, loud on screams … a superstar doing a super performance, right before the eyes of the world.

Honolulu Advertiser

Right: **International Convention Center Arena, Honolulu, January 13–14, 1973**

After a "rehearsal" show on the Friday, Elvis' performance was broadcast live via satellite just after midnight on Saturday night, reaching most countries in the Far East, followed by a delayed link to twenty-eight European countries later that Sunday. Viewers in the United States, however, didn't get to see the show until the following April.

Our marriage was now part-time. He wanted freedom to come and go as he pleased— and he did. When he was home, he was attentive and loving as father and husband. But it was clearly understood that I was mainly responsible for the parenting of Lisa.

Priscilla Presley

Left: **Superior Court, Santa Monica, October 9, 1973**

Hand in hand, Elvis and Priscilla leave the courthouse after being granted a divorce on the grounds of irreconcilable differences. The twenty-minute hearing included an agreement to share custody of Lisa Marie.

Life was interesting at Graceland. There were times when it was like living a fairy tale, you know, and Elvis truly was Prince Charming. He was the most generous of men. He was the kindest, most sensitive, the funniest, most talented, most gorgeous, and sexiest.

Linda Thompson

Right: **With Linda Thompson, 1974**

Ex-Miss Memphis State and Miss Tennessee, Linda Thompson, first dated Elvis in the summer of 1972. After Elvis' divorce Linda became a loyal partner, moving into Graceland and supporting him through increasingly troubled times until their final split at the end of 1976.

I think he really loved Linda, but he just couldn't bring himself to marry her. When he broke up with her it was downhill from then on.

Lowell Hayes, jeweler

Right: **With Linda Thompson, c. 1975**

Throughout the mid-1970s, when his regular partner was Linda Thompson, Elvis continued his long-term passion for karate, elements of which were reflected in the flamboyant choreography of his stage act.

Dr. Nick

"For a long time," Dr. Nick told writer Stanley Booth in 1980, "I didn't realize the full extent of the part I was playing in this thing."

This "thing" was the care and maintenance of Elvis Presley's drug abuse, and of his career. Keeping Elvis alive made it possible for the show to go on, and lots of paychecks depended on that show. Prescription drug addiction was less understood then, and clinics versed in that treatment were rare, particularly for high profile clients. Something that should have been intolerable was simply maintained. "It was a dilemma for me," Dr. Nick said. "It felt like this was going beyond the boundaries of doctoring, and yet it wasn't, because his welfare, his health, were involved, and it's hard to separate that aspect of it from the business aspect."

Dr. George Nichopoulos, a.k.a. "Dr. Nick," has arguably the most infamous name in medicine since Samuel Mudd. He has been lampooned in *The Simpsons*, and there was even an alleged assassination attempt on his life in 1978.

Yet Dr. Nick was praised by close friends of Elvis and by fellow physicians for his empathy and his hyperbolic supervision of Elvis Presley. As detailed by writer Peter Guralnick, he stopped shipments of drugs mailed to Elvis by less scrupulous physicians and was often on call to Elvis for eighteen hours at a time. When Elvis, after an August 1976 disagreement with Dr. Nick, brought a replacement doctor on tour, many noted Elvis' incoherent state; the Colonel begged Dr. Nick to return, and he did. He was indicted in 1979 and 1980 for overprescribing medications for his most famous patient; he was acquitted of the charges both times.

The Medical Examiners Board finally stripped Dr. Nichopoulos of his license in 1996, when he was judged guilty of over-prescribing medicine to thirteen patients, including Jerry Lee

Above: **Graceland, December 28, 1970**

Clockwise from top left, Elvis, Edna Nichopoulus, Dr. Nick, Priscilla Presley, and Lisa Marie.

Lewis. Apparently unable to negotiate the murky waters between saving a drug addict's life and maintaining their lifestyle, Nichopoulus has sought counseling. But Dr. Nick has had numerous patients come forward, claiming he was their last resort, and that he saved them. That resort, at the time of writing, is no longer available.

To keep a drug addict alive and functioning is to maintain a drug addiction; it is a marriage made in hell. Elvis' autopsy found traces of 14 prescription stimulants and depressants in his body. Dr. Nick was as culpable as the rest; more so with his license. But his folkloric status as the King's drug pusher is unfairly conferred; there were too many people unable to say "no" to the King.

Ginger Alden

Elvis' constant companion for the last months of his life was girlfriend Ginger Alden. Here she talks to Andrew Hearn of the *Essential Elvis UK* magazine, telling of her first meeting with Elvis at Graceland:

"[On] the evening of November 19, 1976, George Klein called my sister Terry, the reigning Miss Tennessee, asking if she would like to meet Elvis. My sister was engaged at the time but thought, of course it would be nice to see Graceland and meet Elvis. She told George yes, but felt awkward going alone. My sister, Rosemary, suggested that she and I accompany Terry saying they could always ask us to leave. We arrived at Graceland and were escorted upstairs and in to his daughter Lisa's bedroom. I know this sounds funny, but when Elvis entered the room, I thought trumpets would sound. He looked so handsome. He quickly sat in a chair and started talking with each of us. It turned out to be a truly wonderful evening as he took us on a tour of Graceland. Later he sang for us and read aloud from some of his books about religion."

Left: **Harrison, Arkansas, January 3, 1977**

Elvis with girlfriend Ginger Alden at her grandfather's funeral, to which he had flown Ginger and her family.

He was a great person to dress, he had a terrific build at that point . . . (But) at the time we started in Vegas, everything was Liberace. And I would see these outlandish things with fur and feathers and think, "That's not going to be Elvis. And if that's what he wants, he can get somebody else." I wanted the clothes to be easy and seductive and that was it. And I never wanted anything to compromise his masculinity.

Bill Belew, costume designer

Right: **Jumpsuit, 1970s**

The mastermind of the jumpsuit costumes was Bill Belew, who had first worked with Elvis on his high-collared "Napoleonic" look and black leather suit for the '68 "comeback" TV show.

There was a new look in development for Elvis. We had literally gone as far as we could with the jewels and the embroidery work, and I was working on this new idea: it was a costume with lasers. Between the spotlights hitting the jewels and the lasers coming from the suit, it would have really been spectacular.

Bill Belew

Above and following pages: **Jumpsuits, 1970s**

Bill Belew designed all of Elvis' stage clothes during the 1970s, and many of the jumpsuits had individual names. Overleaf (left) is the red, white, and blue suit designed to commemorate the 1976 US Bicentennial featuring the American eagle in the design, alongside the "phoenix" jumpsuit (right) with its "phoenix rising" motif.

Above: **On stage, fall, 1976**

By the end of 1976 Elvis' increase in weight was very apparent. At the same time, the suits, the sideburns, the sunglasses all contributed to creating the stereotype beloved of Elvis impersonators ever since.

Left: **On stage, 1974**

The "peacock" jumpsuit was one of Elvis' favorite designs. For Elvis, peacocks represented eternal life.

In spite of what you may hear or you may read, we're here, and we're healthy, and we're doing what we enjoy doing.

A tired-looking Elvis addressing the crowd, Kansas City, Missouri, June 18, 1977

Right: **On stage, March 1977**

Throughout the first half of 1977, Elvis' concert appearances became more unpredictable. There were often late showings and even mid-set breaks to answer "nature's call." The star frequently forgot lyrics and uttered rambling, almost incoherent links between songs. Although his fans still adored him, audience reactions and press reviews were beginning to acknowledge that something was seriously wrong with their idol.

Left: **With Vernon on stage, June 1977**

Elvis frequently got his father up on stage to take a bow. Here they are onstage for one of Elvis' last concert appearances.

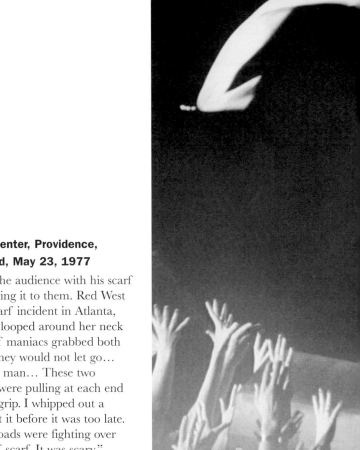

Right: **Civic Center, Providence, Rhode Island, May 23, 1977**

Elvis teases the audience with his scarf before throwing it to them. Red West recalled a scarf incident in Atlanta, Georgia: "It looped around her neck and a pair of maniacs grabbed both ends. Well, they would not let go... She is dying, man... These two broads who were pulling at each end had a death grip. I whipped out a knife and cut it before it was too late. Then the broads were fighting over the shreds of scarf. It was scary."

Mirror

ELVIS PRESLEY IS DEAD

BRITAIN'S BIGGEST DAILY SALE 7p   Wednesday, August 17, 1977

From ANTHONY DELANO in New York

ELVIS Presley, the country boy who became the King of Rock, is dead.

And the superstar who had millions of adoring fans throughout the world was alone when the end came yesterday.

He collapsed yesterday afternoon in the sprawling mansion in Memphis, Tennessee, that he had turned into a fortress against the world.

He was 42, but the excesses of recent years, drugs and compulsive eating, made him look ten years older.

Elvis was a grotesque and obese figure, almost unrecognisable from the lean, gyrating figure of the 1950s.

He was found in the middle of the afternoon by his road manager, Joe Esposito, who gave him the kiss of life.

An ambulance raced Elvis to the Baptist Hospital in Memphis, where he had been recently treated for a liver complaint, eye failure and — it was an open secret — addiction to amphetamines and heroin.

His bodyguards followed the ambulance and broke down in tears as doctors pronounced him dead.

Waiting

Doctors said that Elvis, who had never smoked or drank, may have been dead when he was found lying in the mansion fully dressed on his bed.

"There was no sign of life when he was brought into the hospital," one said.

His personal physician, Dr. George Nichopoulos, was waiting at the hospital.

"Was it drugs that finally struck Elvis down? An overdose?"

Dr. Nichopoulos had no comment. But, the cause of death was

Was King of Rock killed by drugs?

announced by Memphis Director of Police, Winslow Chapman, as "respiratory failure."

Elvis Presley barely survived his birth to become the top selling star of the century. He made more than 30 films during his career, and sold more than 25 million records.

"When he was just a little fellow he would try to sing with the choir," said his mother, Gladys.

When Elvis was 12 Gladys bought him a guitar, which he taught himself to play.

But it was not until 1954, when he was 19 and the family had moved to Memphis that Elvis, then a truck driver, began to demonstrate that "That's All

Right Mama," and the legend was born.

Hits like "Hound Dog," followed. And Elvis became a household name in every language.

Presley's ex-wife, Priscilla, mother of his nine-year-old daughter, Lisa, immediately left for Memphis.

"I am distraught," she said. "I have been phoning Elvis for about a year over his health."

Police said they were investigating to see if drugs were involved in Elvis's death.

His girlfriend Linda Thompson, collapsed in tears. She said: "I saw Elvis only two weeks ago — he had lost a lot of weight and looked fitter than ever."

One of the latest pictures of Elvis. He died from "respiratory failure" aged 42

I can guarantee you one thing; we will never again agree on anything as we agreed on Elvis. So I won't bother saying good-bye to his corpse. I will say good-bye to you.

Writer Lester Bangs on Elvis' death

Left: **The Daily Mirror, August 17, 1977**

Newspapers worldwide carried the story of his death with stark pictures of Elvis' last appearances on stage.

Left: **The Graceland gates, August 17, 1977**

The fans had always lined up at the Graceland gates before Elvis returned home from touring. Now the crowds began to form just as soon as the announcement of his death was made, keeping vigil outside Graceland. Vernon insisted that the funeral be held at home, and that the fans be given the opportunity to view the body. By August 17, 50,000 people filed past Elvis' casket. Telegrams poured in from around the world—B.B. King, Danny Thomas, Little Richard, Isaac Hayes, and hundreds more.

Previous page: **Elvis Presley Boulevard, August 18, 1977**

The two o'clock service in the Graceland living room was attended by family and friends. Ann-Margret and husband Roger Smith were there, as were Chet Atkins and Tennessee governor Ray Blanton. Elvis had always loved the way Kathy Westmoreland sang "Heavenly Father"—she sang it here, with other musical tributes from J.D. Sumner and The Stamps, The Statesmen, Jake Hess, and James Blackwood. The body was then carried in a white hearse, followed by seventeen white limousines, to the chapel of the Forest Hill Cemetery.

Right: **Forest Hill Cemetery, August 18, 1977**

On the morning of August 18, it took one hundred vans four hours to move all the floral displays to the cemetery; in fact, FTD (Floral Transit Delivery) had their single largest sales that day. The local phone company asked that calls be limited to emergencies because the lines were so overloaded. After being interred in a crypt near his mother's grave, Elvis' body and that of his mother were moved to the Meditation Garden at Graceland early in October 1977.

The legacy

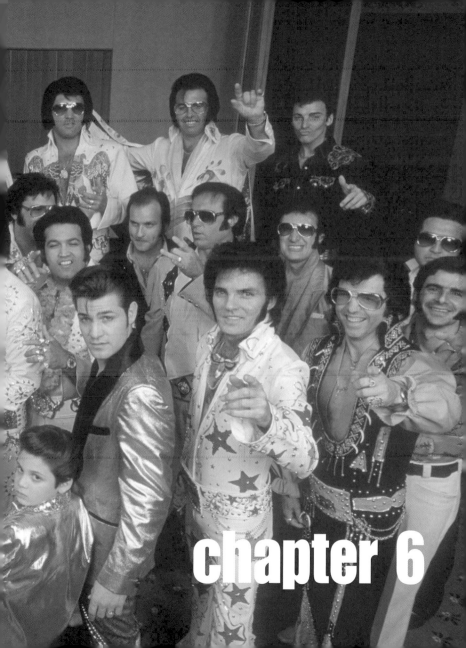

chapter 6

How Great Thou Art

Elvis' post mortem career is as meteoric as his living one, and has already lasted longer. Worldwide, there are more than 600 fan clubs affiliated with Elvis Presley Enterprises—ten times the number there were twenty years ago. At the end of the twentieth century, more than half of Graceland's visitors were under thirty-five, meaning a good many of them were born after his death. The largest fan club is in the UK, with more than 20,000 members; there is also a club in Istanbul and three in Jerusalem.

In 1993, the U.S. Postal Service issued a stamp which bore the face of Elvis Presley. In an unprecedented move, the Postal Service held a ballot to decide which of two pictures—the young Elvis or the Vegas Elvis—would appear. More than a million votes were cast, and 75 percent demanded the young King.

The fact that this ballot was held at all illustrates the eternal duality of the Elvis Presley legend. Even at a point when his image should be most fixed—the issuing of a stamp in his likeness—the two sides of Elvis Presley are brought forth, and laid down for a public verdict. Elvis will always be, like his mama told him, more than one. For every image of Elvis there is a counter image. When one thinks of his remarkable generosity, one is also reminded of his blinding egotism. For every sold out concert there is a shot out television. Every woozy karate move conjures up the slim-hipped swivel of his youth.

Elvis was a nexus of black and white, blues and country, male and female, sex and androgyny. When he got up on the stage in 1954 all of those facets shimmered in him, whichever way the light hit him. What pundits and politicians represented as sexual threat was actually the unfinished nature of Elvis.

Elvis had endured the humiliating effects of poverty, his father's incarceration and never-ending quests for a new job, a new home, a better life that was always just out of reach. He was a mama's boy, told continually that he was better than everyone else. He built a private world where he was king, where his social and economic superiors would bow to his sovereignty. He traveled in this private realm; it accompanied him when he saw Mississippi Slim perform, when he gazed hungrily into the windows of Lansky's, while he daydreamed his classes away in high school, when he worked desultorily at the typical teenage jobs in Memphis.

And then his dreams, improbably and impossibly, came true. They plunged him into a world that seemed like a dream, where all his fantasies bore gorgeous and horrible fruit. His mother, who had bred this dream of greatness in him, died just as these dreams had overtaken their lives—in a state of bewilderment.

John Lennon had proclaimed that, "Elvis died the day he went into the army." It didn't help that Elvis acquired a pill habit that would further steer the naïve young star down a road of isolation, temper tantrums, and bloated self-esteem which alternated with a deep sense of inferiority. However, Elvis, and all he meant to us, didn't die when he entered the army. Films killed Elvis: they neutered him, rubbed off the rough edges of insecurity and sexual threat that radiated from him on the stage and in the studio. They turned him into a *nice guy*, a guy who sang to children, puppets, bulls. They turned him into a forty-foot image with flawless pores and whose reactions were as predictable and tame as his increasingly shellacked hair. They made him into the kind of kid that Memphis could be proud of.

When Elvis returned to live touring he shimmered once again, but it was a different light. This Elvis, bejeweled and dazzling, reflected back the fans' gaze and memory. He could project from them the youthful, dangerous Elvis, the Elvis that had cried over his mother's coffin, the Elvis that had shuffled and grinned through thirty-one schlocky movies, the Elvis that had emerged from the '68 special triumphing over a vitiated career (and over age itself, it seemed), the Elvis that was enshrouded in the glitz and glamor of Vegas—the apex of American luxury and vulgarity, the Elvis that was self-destructing. Every performance now told the story of Elvis: with every beautiful song, with every terrible song, with the surprising litheness he still showed, with the pants that he split, with the monologues that charmed or embarrassed his audience, depending on his health or sobriety.

His story was told so many times that just a word can revive the whole. The story of Elvis is the story of democracy, as Greil Marcus observed in his essay "Elvis: Presliad":

"Elvis takes his strength from the liberating arrogance, pride, and the claim to be unique that grow out of a rich and commonplace understanding of what 'democracy' and 'equality' are all about: No man is better than I am. He takes his strength as well from the humility, the piety, and the open, self-effacing good humor that spring from the same source: I am better than no man."

Peter Guralnick also notes the remarkable osmosis between Elvis the everyman and Elvis the king: "Everywhere you go you can see Elvis as he might have been." Aviator sunglasses or big sideburns can transform anyone into Elvis—that's why Elvis impersonators flourish. But each evocation also reminds us of how unique he was. Because at the center of this phenomenon there is still a moment of stillness: that moment when he shuffled or strode into Sun Studio; when he sang "That's All Right" with an artistry and hubris that was a shot in the dark. A shot heard around the world. A shot that stopped the heart beating and then restarted it in a whole new way.

Elvis was the king. No doubt about it. People like myself, Mick Jagger, and all the others only followed in his footsteps.

Rod Stewart

Above: **The Meditation Garden, Graceland**

Elvis' grave in the Meditation Garden, flanked by those of his grandmother Minnie Mae (left), father Vernon (right), and mother Gladys (far right).

Left: **The Meditation Garden, Graceland, August 1996**

During the annual Elvis Week commemoration of Elvis' death, his grave in the Meditation Garden at Graceland is covered in floral tributes by fans from all over the world. The scale and nature of this almost religious devotion stands alone in the posthumous following of any star of recent times.

Elvis is the greatest cultural force in the twentieth century. He introduced the beat to everything, music, language, clothes. It's a whole new social revolution.

Leonard Bernstein

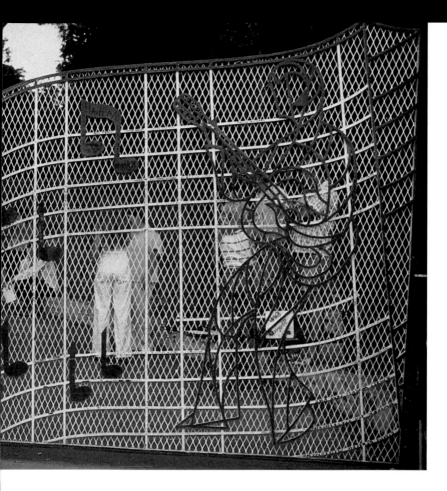

Above: **3764 Elvis Presley Boulevard, Memphis, c. 2000**

The ornamental gates to Graceland have long been a significant gathering place for Elvis pilgrims visiting the mansion.

Without Elvis Presley history would certainly have been different. Jagger might have become an estate agent, Dylan a rabbi, Lennon a bricklayer or Johnny Rotten a judge. He probably was one of the tiny handful of artists who actually affected the course of human affairs.

Mick Farren, writer

Left: **Meditation Garden, August 16, 1985**

One legend honors another: the boxing champion Muhammad Ali pays a visit to Elvis' gravesite on the eighth anniversary of the singer's death.

He could have started a religion. In a way, he did.
Nick Tosches, writer

Right: **Downtown, Memphis**

Elvis is recognized by mainstream society for the contribution he made to the fabric of our culture. This statue of Elvis, seen here looking over downtown Memphis from the west end of Beale Street, has since been moved indoors to the Tennessee Welcome Center which provides tourist information about Memphis and the Beale Street Historic District. The statue now stands next to that of another king, blues musician B.B. King.

Above: **Graceland, unveiling of postage stamp, June 4, 1992**

Sam Phillips looks at a poster of the special Elvis Presley US postage stamp, at a ceremony at Graceland announcing the winning design.

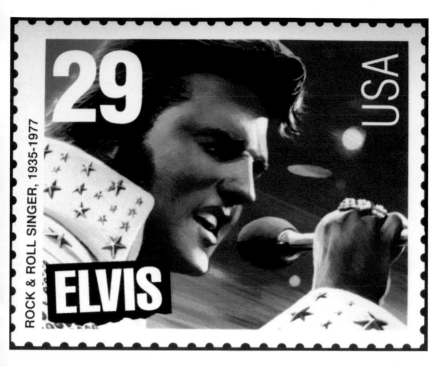

Above: **Elvis stamp, 1992**

After more than 1.2 million ballots were submitted by fans, the choice was made by a margin of 3 to 1 for the "younger" Elvis picture to be used on the stamp, rather than this image from his "Las Vegas" period.

Redemption

At the time of Elvis' death, his finances were in serious trouble. He would, occasionally, mortgage Graceland to make the payroll. While much of that can be attributed to Elvis' reckless spending habits, the Colonel's portion of Elvis' earnings was sometimes up to 70 percent. While Elvis' body lay in his coffin, the Colonel convinced Vernon to sign a deal allowing Parker to continue making 50 percent from the King's estate. After Vernon's death in 1979, Priscilla Presley became the executor of the estate and, in 1982, the estate challenged Colonel Parker's hold over Elvis' earnings. An out-of-court settlement eliminated the Colonel's future share of Elvis' income, and prevented him from commercially exploiting the Presley name for five years.

That same year also heralded the opening of Graceland to the public, which helped build Elvis Presley Enterprises into a fifteen-million-dollar-a-year business. A quarter of a century after his death, Elvis continues to sell more records dead than most acts manage to when alive. In 2003, for the third year in a row according to *Forbes* magazine, Elvis was the top-earning dead celebrity—all Elvis-related materials raked in some $40 million, adding to the Presley estate's estimated worth of $250 million.

It wasn't just the King's finances that were in trouble in 1977. The image of a bloated and drug-ridden recluse had all but eclipsed the young man who changed music history. Starting with the book released in the summer of his death—Elvis: What Happened?—a slew of confessional, tabloid-style tomes were dumped upon a hungry public. For the next decade anyone with anything negative to say about Elvis was given the podium, while any defense of Elvis was remarkably muted. It was perhaps the inevitable destiny of one who was so worshipped.

The culmination of these literary autopsies was the widely

read Elvis by the widely loathed Albert Goldman, a biography which gleefully savaged what was left of Elvis' good name. Happily, the pendulum has swung back. Many books and essays have tried to understand Elvis Presley and what he meant to popular culture and history. No author approached that goal with more empathy and rigor than writer Peter Guralnick, whose two books Last Train to Memphis: The Rise of Elvis Presley and Careless Love: The Unmaking of Elvis Presley, have achieved new heights in Elvisology and music biography.

"I heard the news," Elvis would sing in "Good Rockin' Tonight"—but he was the news.
Greil Marcus, writer

Next page: **Graceland, 2004**

The most spectacular display in the exhibition spaces at Graceland is that devoted to Elvis Presley's gold and platinum records and other awards, plus the definitive collection of Elvis jumpsuits from the 1970s.

Elvis was the King of rock'n'roll because he was the embodiment of its sins and virtues: grand and vulgar, rude and eloquent, powerful and frustrated, absurdly simple and awesomely complex.

Dave March, Rolling Stone

Left: **Joni Mabe, 1990s**

Installation artist and lifelong Elvis fanatic, Joni Mabe has traveled the world with her exhibition of Elvis memorabilia and ephemera, consisting of more than 30,000 items, many with the emphasis on the kitsch aspect of Presley worship. Among the more bizarre artifacts on display in the exhibit, which is now permanently housed in Cornelia, Georgia, are a clipping allegedly from Elvis' little toenail, and an Elvis wart preserved in formaldehyde!

Above: **Marion Keisker, 1984**

Seen here holding an Elvis doll, Marion Keisker was Sam Phillips' assistant at Sun Records who first heard Elvis when he came into the Memphis Recording Service in July 1953 to make a two-sided acetate at his own expense, singing "My Happiness" and "That's When Your Heartaches Begin." Keisker was instrumental in drawing Phillips' attention to the young hopeful, and in doing so played a key role in the early evolution of rock'n'roll music.

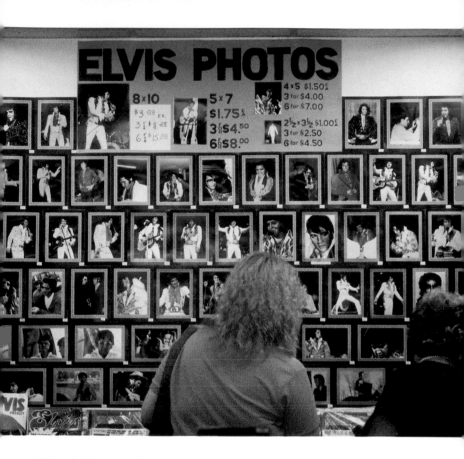

Above: **Elvis photos on sale**

From the bedroom walls of teenagers in the 1950s to the collections of countless thousands of fans and enthusiasts today, Elvis' image—in all its many manifestations—is still much sought after.

Elvis auction

Above: **Elvis memorabilia, Las Vegas auction, 1999**

Elvis memorabilia has appeared over the years in various auction sales. The largest was in October 1999, the "Official Auction" of material from the Elvis Presley archives at Graceland, which was held in Las Vegas. A portion of the proceeds went to a Memphis housing project called Presley Place. The sale included original performance contracts and letters from the collection of Colonel Tom Parker.

Time has a way of being very unkind to old records, but Elvis' keep getting better and better.

Huey Lewis, singer

Below: **Elvis Army fatigue, Las Vegas auction, 1999**

One of Elvis' items of clothing from his time in the army which went on sale at the Graceland archive auction held in Las Vegas in 1999.

Above: **Decorated guitar, date unknown**

Not just memorabilia from Elvis' life and times, but items designed since as "souvenirs" of the memory of the King—such as this decorated guitar—have become collectibles in their own right.

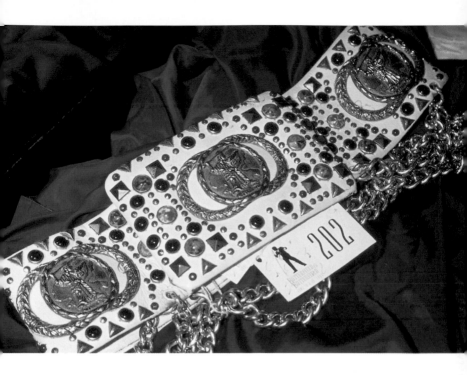

Above: **Stage suit belt, 1970s**

One of the items sold at the 1999 auction was this decorative belt, typical of many worn by Elvis in his "jumpsuit" period in the 1970s.

Interview with Bill Haney
(Elvis impersonator)

Interview by Tom Graves, Memphis, 1996

In 1976, pioneering Elvis impersonator Bill Haney was paid the highest compliment of all: a surprise visit to his show by Elvis himself. Impressed by what he saw, Elvis invited the entertainer to Graceland for a visit. Haney recalls the evening:

One night after my show at the Levee Lounge in Memphis, the manager come up to me and asked me, "Do you know who was here just a while ago?" I shook my head and the manager says "Elvis." I looked at that manager and says, "Man, you're kidding me."

He says, "Naw, man."

And I says, "Holy s**t."

And the manager says, "Elvis was sittin' right back there in that booth. I let them in through the kitchen 'cause they called before they came and told me what they wanted. They didn't want any attention, they wanted lights out, and they wanted back in a dark corner somewhere."

And that's what they did. They turned the lights out in the booth— several booths, actually—and he came in with a cowboy hat on, sat in the back with the lights all out. Nobody even knew he was there and there was people all around him. It's probably a good thing I didn't know about him being there. I probably would've got all tongue-tied on the stage.

Charlie Hodge had stayed behind and the manager brings him around. Charlie says, "Hey man, where you want me to pick you up?"

I says, "What you mean?"

And he says, "You do want to meet Elvis, don't you?"

I says, "Oh, hell yeah."

And Charlie says, "Elvis told me to stay and bring you out to the house for a while."

So we started over there to Graceland and I thought that was great, but the impact didn't hit me until those gates opened up and we started up the drive and I thought, "Holy s**t! I'm really gonna meet this guy!" You know, hundreds and hundreds, millions of people would like to meet him, and here I am going in to meet him.

I went in the house, and Elvis was upstairs and me and Charlie messed around in the Jungle Room, Charlie joking around and stuff. Finally, Charlie says, "Hey man, c'mere, c'mere, Elvis is coming down the stairs."

Charlie introduced me to him and Elvis stuck out his left hand and said, "Excuse my right hand, man, I've got a burn." I couldn't help but notice that his left hand was just full of diamonds. Both his hands were unusually puffy. Soft, puffy. He says to me, "Hey man, come on outside. I wanta show you my motherf*****g cars." We went outside and there was a brand new Lincoln Mark IV. He had just given away five brand new Marks to people. He looks at me and says, "Ain't this one a motherf****r, man?" And I said, "Yeah man, that is nice." He made me feel pretty easy. We sat around in the house for a long time just talkin', jokin', and playin' with the dogs. Charlie was cuttin' up and asks him, "Elvis, what do think about ol' Haney?" Elvis looks at me and laughs and says, "I like his style."

It was like there was some damn aura around the guy. I've never met anybody who projected that type of electricity. I've met a lot of stars in my lifetime ... Jerry Lee Lewis, Roy Orbison, Johnny Cash, Ricky Nelson ... and he is more different than anybody. I never met anything like Presley. And never will.

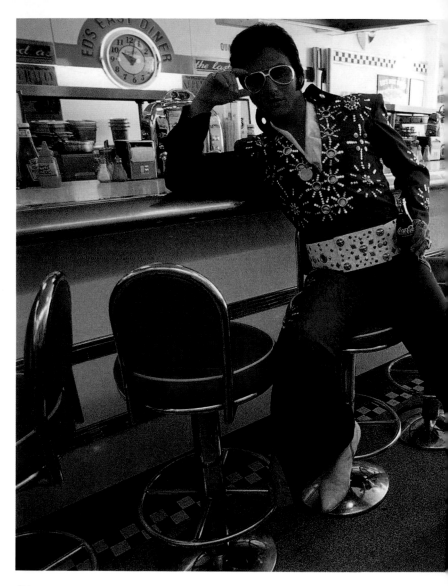

Left: **Elvis impersonator, London, 1990s**

Clayton Mark, a Las Vegas Elvis impersonator, sitting in a '50s-style American diner in London, where he now lives. In 1991 he staged *Memories of Elvis* with a 14-piece band based on Elvis' Las Vegas Hilton appearance in 1971, and also appeared in the London stage show *Elvis: The Musical*.

Following page: **Stars In Their Eyes, 1992**

Comedian Russ Abbott (front row, center) introduced no less than eleven Elvis lookalikes on the UK talent show *Stars In Their Eyes* in which members of the public impersonate musical celebrities.

If life were fair, Elvis would be alive and all the impersonators would be dead.

Johnny Carson, TV host

Right: **The People newspaper, October 6, 1996**

"Elvis lives" rumors and urban myths, like this one in a UK newspaper in 1996, began to circulate soon after the day he died, and still persist to this day.

55p   October 6, 1996

THE People

NATIONAL NEWSPAPER OF THE YEAR   SUNDAY NEWSPAPER OF THE YEAR

TV **FIRST**

FREE with The People

Your programme for the week of Oct 6-12

GUESS WHO ISN'T COMING TO DINNER!
Coronation Street, ITV,
Monday, Wednesday, Friday

FREE TAPE!

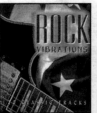

ROCK VIBRATIONS

20 CLASSIC TRACKS

20 HOT ROCK HITS
FOR EVERY READER!

FREE INSIDE

THE BEST 7–DAY TV GUIDE

ELVIS IS ALIVE!

WORLD EXCLUSIVE

For the first time his cousin tells of Elvis's secret escape on the night a shattered world was told 'The King Is Dead'

SEE PAGES 4 and 5

WIN CARS AND CASH

See Yes! magazine

k: 2120649d

413

Above: **Graceland, Memphis, 1996**

In many ways the graffiti outside Graceland says it all, the image of Elvis transcending fashion or styles of music. It has become a cultural icon in its own right.

Right: **Graceland, Memphis, 1996**

Elvis fans hold a candlelit vigil outside Graceland to mark the anniversary of his death, August, 1996.

Above: **Graceland, August 15, 2002**

The "Elvis Week" commemorations of his death were bigger than usual on the 25th anniversary in 2002. Here fans file respectfully past his grave during the candlelight vigil.

Following page: **25th Anniversary Concert, August 16, 2002**

Based on a spectacular show which has toured the world, a 25th Anniversary concert in Memphis had Elvis' original Las Vegas band playing to "live" video projections of the King in action.

Before Elvis, there was nothing.

John Lennon

Photo Credits

Thanks to the following for help with image sourcing:
Andrew Croft, Donna Gosling, Andrew Hearn, Russ Howe,
Joseph Krein, Donna Russell.

Fotos International/Rex Features
front cover image

The Associated Press
pages 12–13, 51, 338, 346, 374-375, 388, 392, 393 (US Postal Service).

Beatlology Magazine, www.beatlology.com
p. 261

CORBIS
pages 5, 36–37, 47, 61, 62-63, 105, 119, 242; © **Bettmann/Corbis:** pages
59, 72–73, 106, 107, 108-109, 128, 130, 131, 139, 154, 163, 165, 182–183,
187, 214–215, 275, 279, 280–281, 368–369; © **Kevin Fleming/Corbis:**
pages 384, 414, 415; © **Ralf-Finn Hestoft/Corbis SABA:** p. 378–379; ©
Seattle Museum of History & Industry/Corbis: p. 232

Essential Elvis UK, www.essentialelvis.com
pages 97, 208, 223, 247, 320, 353, 354

Elvis2001 Archives, www.elvis2001.net
pages 113, 231, 233, 257

Getty Images
pages 20, 124–125, 176, 416–417, 419; **CBS Photo Archive/Getty
Images © 2003 CBS Worldwide Inc.:** p. 123; **Time Life
Pictures/Getty Images:** pages 35, 86, 88-89, 90–91, 114, 166–167, 169,
171, 172–173, 188, 189, 190–191

Mirrorpix
pages 370, 408, 410–411, 413

MQ Publications
pages 31, 57

US National Archives [Nixon Presidential Materials Staff (NLNS), National Archives at College Park, MD]
p. 330

Redferns
Glenn A. Baker Archives/Redferns: pages 42, 49, 66–67, 132, 264;
Michael Ochs Archives/Redferns: pages 35, 56, 98–99, 133, 134, 142, 153, 217, 272–273, 295, 321, 325, 342; **Steve Morley/Redferns:** p. 332;
Charlyn Zlotnik/Redferns: p. 359

Rex Features
pages 143, 213, 256, 349, 386–387, 401; **Peter Brooker/Rex Features:** pages 404, 405; **Everett Collection/Rex Features:** pages 8–9, 23, 25, 29, 83, 84, 96, 102–103, 110, 111, 118, 121, 126, 140, 145, 158, 161, 168, 175, 177, 192–193, 204, 207, 210–211, 212, 218, 221, 224, 225, 227, 228, 229, 230, 234, 244–245, 248, 249, 250–251, 252–253, 255, 259, 262, 266, 268, 269, 270–271, 274, 277, 282, 284, 286, 287, 289, 290, 297, 298–299, 301, 316, 317, 322–323, 326, 328, 329, 333–334, 336–337, 343, 357, 361, 366–367; **Brian Rasic, Everything Elvis/Rex Features:** p. 398; **Fotos International/Rex Features:** pages 159, 302–303, 345; **Richard Gardner/Rex Features:** pages 147, 396–397; **Globe Photos Inc./Rex Features:** pages 26, 27, 95, 319, 362, 365; **Images/Rex Features:** p. 360; **Sipa Press/Rex Features:** pages 2, 138, 179, 219, 372–373, 377, 391, 400, 402; **Snap/Rex Features:** pages 55, 71, 92, 112, 116–117, 136–137, 141, 146, 148–149, 151, 155, 156, 236, 238–239, 241, 258, 263, 292–293, 294, 363; **Stills Press Agency/Rex Features:** pages 101, 180–181; **Today/Rex Features:** p. 403; **Steve Ward/Rex Features:** p. 385

Acknowledgments

Many thanks to Rose Clayton, author of *Elvis: By Those Who Knew Him Best* for her initial encouragement. Many books have been written about Elvis Presley, but Peter Guralnick's two part biography, *Last Train to Memphis* and *Careless Love*, rises above the herd. I thank him for his work on Elvis, which helped me enormously in the writing of this book. Kudos to Mike Evans, who really pulled this book together and whose patient good humor softened every deadline.

Thank you to my dear husband Robert Gordon for all his editing, computer savvy, and support. Nothing could be done without you.

Thanks to Lila and Esther for being my sweet children and for not fighting too much when I was busy.

Quotation Credits

Quoted material comes from the following sources:

p14 "My daddy may…" *Last Train to Memphis*, by Peter Guralnick, hereafter referred to as Guralnick 1

p15 "They entered me…" *TV Radio Mirror* 1956

p15 "Son, wouldn't you…" *TV Radio Mirror* 1956

p19 "One of the problems…" *Elvis!: The Last Word*, by Sandra Choron and Bob Oskam hereafter referred to as Choron

p21 "Though we had friends…" *Good Housekeeping*, January 1978

p22 "East Tupelo, Mississippi…" *Elvis By Those Who Knew Him Best*, by Rose Clayton and Dick Heard, hereafter referred to as Clayton

p28 "We were broke…" Commercial Appeal March 7, 1955

p32 "I have an opinion…" interview by Tom Graves

p34 "During our dating days…" Choron

p41 "The odd thing about it…" Memphis Press Scimitar, 1954

p41 "I was scared stiff…" *Elvis: A 30-Year Chronicle*, Bill E. Burk

p41 "I don't think…" Guralnick 1

p46 "This cat came out…" Guralnick 1

p54 "It was a mixture…" Choron

p58 "When Elvis came to Florida…" Clayton

p64 "Parker was ahead..." Clayton

p64 "He looked…" Guralnick 1

p65 "Well, about a year…" Clayton

p68 "Anytime anyone was different…" Clayton

p70 "When Elvis started…" Clayton

p74 "Jackie Gleason loved…" Clayton

p79 "Elvis cried…" Clayton

p80 "I knew what it was…" Guralnick 1

p80 "Everything I have…" Guralnick 1

p82 "I remember when…" Choron

p85 "Everything happened so blame fast..." *The King On The Road*, Robert Gordon, hereafter referred to as Gordon

p87 "I didn't know..." Guralnick 1

p93 "Thick-lipped, droopy-eyed..." *New Yorker* magazine, November 1956

p100 "Goddamn it, shit!…" Guralnick 1

p100 "like a jug…" *Newsweek*, May 14, 1956

p104 "The booking was..." *Down At The End of Lonely Street*, Peter Brown and Pat Broeske, hereafter referred to as Brown

p104 "For teenagers..." *Variety*, May 1956

p113 "You know those people..." *Elvis Day By Day*, Peter Guralnick and Ernst Jorgensen

p115 "I can't figure out..." Brown

p120 "This is a real decent..." *Elvis Day By Day*, Peter Guralnick and Ernst Jorgensen

p122 "On the Sullivan programme..." *New York Times*, September 10, 1956

p127 "He's a real pixie..." *Tupelo Daily Journal*, 13 September 1956

p129 "Mr. Presley's first..." *New York Times*, November 1956

p135 "Elvis Presley's second..." *Variety*, July 1957

p144 "the darkest blue…" *Memphis Press Scimitar*, March 26, 1957

p144 "There is also a story…" *Elvis and Gladys*, Elaine Dundy,

p150 "This time most..." *New York Times*, November 1957

p152 "We'll fill in…" Guralnick 1

p153 "We never worked…" Guralnick 1

p157 "The part gives him..." *News Chronicle*, July 1958

p162 "The army can do..." Memphis Press-Scitar, March 24, 1958

p164 "Elvis arrived..." Choron

p170 "I had to get used..." *New York Journal-American*, June 21, 1959

p174 "It may surprise you..." Choron

p178 "He sat on his butt..." Choron

p184 "He flat-out attacked…" Brown

p196 "I was asked…" *Careless Love*, Peter Guralnick, hereafter referred to as Guralnick 2

p197 "Don't let's get…" *Elvis and Me*, Priscilla Presley

p203 "There is something magical…" Elvis.com/Elvisology

p206 "Rock'n'roll is sung..." *Anti-Rock*, Linda Martin and Kerry Seagrave

p209 "Man, I got butterflies…' Brown

p216 "It was great for…" Hal Wallis Collection, Academy Library

p220 "What really surprised me…" Choron

p222 "We got off the plane…" Gordon

p222 "The generosity and…" Gordon

p223 "Elvis is a musical…" *Honolulu Advertiser*, March 27 1961

p226 "It's a relief..." *Sunday Telegraph*, May 1962

p235 "Compared with the Beatles..." *New York Times*, November 1963

p237 "We shot the picture…" Clayton

p240 "Music ignited a firey..." *Ann-Margret: My Story*, Ann-Margret,

p244 "Would you believe..." *Las Vegas Desert News and Telegram*, April 20, 1964

p246 "Elvis swung the bus…" *If I Can Dream*, Larry Geller

p252 "I certainly havn't lost..." Memphis *Commercial Appeal*, March 7, 1965

p254 "[Sam Katzman] was..." Clayton

p260 "To be honest..." *Speaking Words of Wisdom*, Spencer Leigh

p270 "He [Elvis] was most..." Clayton

p276 "We were in Nashville…" Clayton

p278 "This is the greatest..." UPI dispatch, July 13, 1967

p280 "He sorta waved…" Clayton

p283 "Elvis hated..." Clayton

p285 "This, after all..." *New York Times*, June 1968

p288 "It was the finest music…" *Mystery Train*, Greil Marcus

p291 "I want to tour…" Guralnick 2

p296 "I was sort of embarrassed..." Guralnick 2

p298 "He confessed..." *After All*, Mary Tyler Moore

p307 "Go out there…" Guralnick 2

p309 "…if I find or hear…" Guralnick 2

p310 "smelled green peppers…" Guralnick 2

p310 "You know, all he can do now is die." Guralnick 2

p311 "We were all wearing blinders..." www.elvis.com.au

p311 "He was like a mirror..." Guralnick 2

p312 "A little nervous..." *Elvis Day By Day*, Peter Guralnick and Ernst Jorgensen

p315 "When I got out…" Quoted in "Elvis Presley: Wagging His Tail In Las Vegas" David Dalton, *Rolling Stone*, 21 February 1970

p318 "A live concert…" *New York Times*, October 11, 1970

p324 "You talk to…" Choron

p327 "You have no idea…" elvis.com/elvisology

p330 "I can and will..." *The Day Elvis Met Nixon*, Egil "Bud" Krogh

p333 "All he needs…" "Elvis Presley: The Cobo Hall, Detroit, Michigan" *Phonograph Record*, Greg Shaw, December 1972

p339 "He would strike..." *Variety*, June 1972

p340 "He came up with…" Guralnick 2

p340 "But when that…" Clayton

p344 "It was a thrilling…" *Honolulu Advertiser*, January 1973

p347 "Our marriage was now…" *Elvis and Me*, Priscilla Presley

p348 "Life was interesting…" Clayton

p350 "I think he really…" Clayton

p352 "For a long time…" *Elvis Reader*, Kevin Quain, hereafter referred to as Quain

p355 "On the evening…" *Essential Elvis UK*

p356 "He was a great…" "The Man Who Dressed the King", Mike Thomas, www.salon.com

p358 "There was a new look..." Clayton

p364 "In spite of what..." *Elvis Day By Day*, Peter Guralnick and Ernst Jorgensen

p368 "It looped around her neck…" *Elvis: What Happened?*, Red West

p371 "I can guarantee…" Quain

p382 "Elvis takes his strength…" *Mystery Train*, Greil Marcus

p382 "Everywhere you go…" *Lost Highway*, Peter Guralnick

p383 "Elvis was the king…" Choron

p386 "Elvis is the greatest…" Choron

p389 "Without Elvis…" *New Musical Express*, Mick Farren, 27 August 1977

p390 "He could have…" Quain

p395 "I heard the news…" Quain

p399 "Elvis was the King…" *Rolling Stone*, Dave Marsh, quoted in Brown/Broeske

p403 "Time has a way…" Choron

p406 "One night after my show…" interview by Tom Graves

p412 "If life were fair..." Choron

p418 "Before Elvis..." Choron

BIBLIOGRAPHY

Burk, Bill E., *Early Elvis: The Tupelo Years*, Propwash: Memphis, 1994
  Elvis: Through My Eyes, Burk Enterprises: Memphis, 1987
Brown, Peter, and Pat Broeske, *Down At The End Of Lonely Street*, Random House (US), 1997
Clayton, Rose, and Dick Heard, *Elvis: By Those Who Knew Him Best*, Virgin Publishing, Ltd., London, 2003
Choron, Sandra, and Bob Oskam, *Elvis!: The Last Word*, New York, Citadel Press, 1991
Crenshaw, Marshall, *Hollywood Rock: A Guide to Rock'N'Roll In the Movies*, New York, HarperCollins, 1994
Dundy, Elaine, *Elvis and Gladys*, New York, Macmillan, 1985
Escott, Colin, with Martin Hawkins, *Good Rockin' Tonight: Sun Records and the Birth of Rock'N'Roll*, New York, St. Martin's, 1991
Geller, Larry, *If I Can Dream: Elvis' Own Story*, New York, Simon and Schuster, 1989
Gordon, Robert, *The King on the Road: Elvis Live on Tour: 1954–1977*, New York, St. Martin's, 2001
  The Elvis Treasures, New York, Random House, 2002
Guralnick, Peter, *Careless Love: The Unmaking of Elvis Presley*, Boston, Little, Brown, 1999
  Feel Like Going Home: Portraits in Blues and Rock'n'Roll, Outerbridge and Dienstfrey, 1971. Reprint, New York, Little, Brown, 1999
  Last Train to Memphis: The Rise of Elvis Presley, Boston, Little, Brown, 1994
  Lost Highway: Journeys and Arrivals of American Musicians, Boston: D. R. Godine, 1979. Reprint, New York: Little, Brown, 1999
  and Ernst Jorgensen, *Elvis Day by Day: The Definitive Record of His Life and Music*, Ballantine, New York, 1999
Hopkins, Jerry, *Elvis, A Biography*, New York, Warner Books, 1975
Marcus, Greil, *Mystery Train: Images of America in Rock'N'Roll Music*, Penguin: New York, 1990
  Dead Elvis: A Chronicle of a Cultural Obsession, New York: Doubleday, 1991
Moore, Mary Tyler, *After All*, Putnam, New York, 1995

Presley, Priscilla Beaulieu, with Sandra Harmon, *Elvis and Me*, New York, G. P. Putnam's Sons, 1985

Quain, Kevin, ed., *The Elvis Reader: Texts and Sources on the King of Rock 'N'Roll*, New York, St. Martin's, 1992

West, Red, Sonny West, Dave Hebler, and Steve Dunleavy, *Elvis: What Happened?*, New York, Ballantine Books, 1977

Other resources

Multimedia:

Elvis 1956, Produced and Directed by Alan Raymond and Susan Raymond, Warner Home Video, 1987. Videocassette.

Elvis on Tour, Produced and Directed by Pierre Adidge and Robert Abel, Turner Entertainment, 1972. Videocassette.

Elvis: That's the Way It Is, Produced by Herbert F. Solow, Directed by Denis Sanders, MGM/UA Home Video, 1970. Videocassette.

Websites:

www.Elvis.com/Elvisology/quotes/aboutelvis.asp

www.geocities.com/ep_first/mediaf/2002/200208c.html

www.elvis.com.au/presley/biography/elvis_presley_biography_1970_1972.shtml

www.robertchristgau.com/xg/bkrev/elvis-97.php

www.epgold.com/index.html

www.theatlantic.com/issues/81jan/demott.htm

www.salon.com/ent/feature/2002/08/16/elvis_death_25/index1.html

http://usuarios.lycos.es/elvistcb/

www.bankrate.com/smm/news/advice/20040108a1.asp

Index

Page references in *italics* indicate illustration captions

265, 276
Juanico, June 76, 79

First published by MQ Publications Limited
12 The Ivories
6–8 Northampton Street
London, N1 2HY
email: mqpublications.com
website: www.mqpublications.com

Editor: Mike Evans

ISBN (10): 1-84072-673-3
ISBN (13): 978-1-84072-673-2

10 9 8 7 6 5 4 3 2

Printed in China

★ 1961

Feb 25 — Elvis performs at the Ellis Auditorium in his hometown.

Mar 25 — At a special charity performance in Honolulu, Elvis raises over $62,000 toward completing the U.S.S. Arizona memorial for the victims of Pearl Harbor.

★ 1962

Dec 19 — Priscilla Beaulieu flies in from Germany to spend Christmas with Elvis in Memphis.

★ 1963

May 29 — Priscilla graduates from Immaculate Conception High School.

★ 1964

April 30 — Elvis meets hairdresser Larry Geller, who will become an important spiritual advisor to Elvis for the next several years.

★ 1965

Aug 27 — The Beatles visit Elvis at his Bel Air home in California.

Sept 30 — Elvis meets Tom Jones.

★ 1966

May — In Nashville, Elvis begins recording his first nonsoundtrack album in two and a half years, *How Great Thou Art*.

Dec — Elvis proposes to Priscilla.

★ 1967

Feb 8 — Elvis purchases a 163 acre cattle ranch which will soon become a home and retreat for Elvis and his friends.

May 1 — Elvis marries Priscilla.

July 12 — Elvis announces that Priscilla is pregnant.

★ 1968

Feb 1 — Exactly nine months after their wedding, Priscilla and Elvis have a daughter—Lisa Marie Presley.

Dec 3 — *SINGER Presents Elvis* is a critical and commercial success. The NBC broadcast becomes forever known as the "68 Comeback Special."

★ 1969

Jan 13 — Elvis begins sessions in Memphis at American Studio. The hits include "In the Ghetto," "Suspicious Minds," "Don't Cry, Daddy," and "Kentucky Rain."

Aug 28 — A ground-breaking performance at the International Hotel Showroom. The 2,200-seat auditorium is filled.

★ 1970

Feb 27 — Elvis performs six shows at the Houston Astrodome.

Jul-Sep — The Vegas documentary *Elvis—That's The Way It Is* is filmed.

Sept — For the first time since 1957, Elvis embarks on a tour of one-nighters.